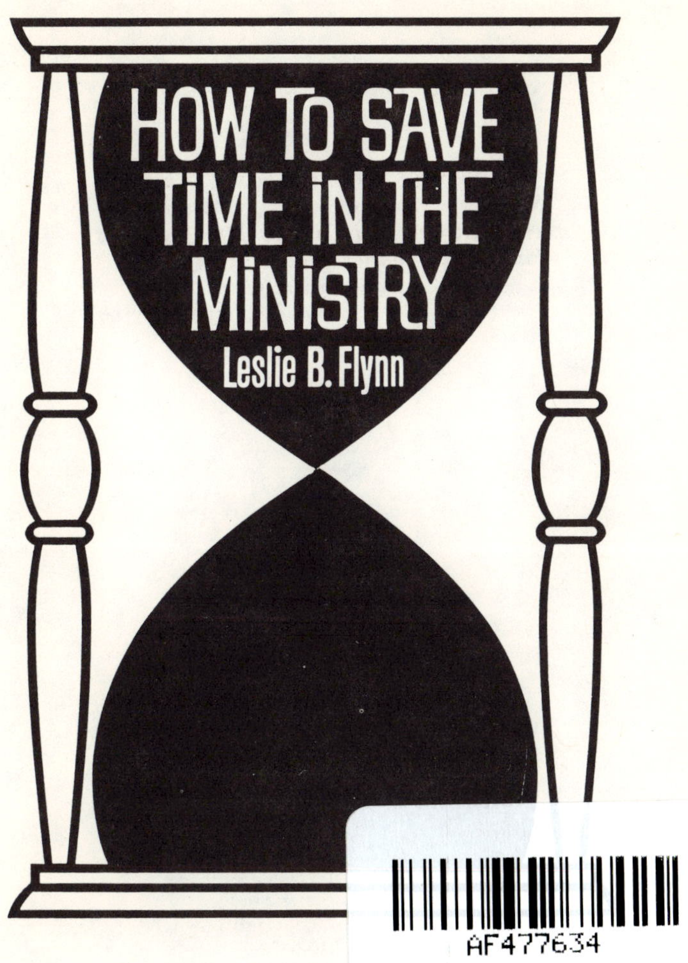

BAKER BOOK HOUSE
Grand Rapids, Michigan

©1966 by Broadman Press
Paperback edition issued 1975
by Baker Book House
with permission of copyright owner
ISBN: 0-8010-3470-1

DEWEY DECIMAL CLASSIFICATION 253.2
Library of Congress catalog card number: 65-23049
Printed in the United States of America
2.MH706

Preface

Today's minister is expected to be a jack-of-all-trades: scholar, financier, visitor, public relations expert, organizer, administrator, preacher, typist, counselor, teacher, social worker, file clerk, correspondent, journalist, educator, real estate agent, and director of the duplicator.

Most pastors carry a work load heavier than they can efficiently handle. One said, "I could work day and night for weeks and not get done all the things I'm supposed to do."

Clergymen do not wish to avoid work but would like to work more efficiently. Experts in the field of human efficiency tell us that most executives work at only one half their potential. Pastors, likewise, could accomplish much more—and with no more effort. The solution is not found in any magic, push-button formula. But hard work harnessed to simple, time-saving methods will enable ministers to stay on top of their work instead of frantically sinking beneath the load.

One board president phrased it, "Work smarter, not harder." The suggestions outlined in this book should help pastors to get more done in fewer hours, thereby ridding themselves of many irritations, pressures, frustrations, and the nagging anxiety of unfinished jobs.

9:00 to 9:15 A.M.

I've dusted my desk and I've wound up my watch,
I've tightened (then loosened) my belt by a notch.
I've polished my glasses, removed a small speck.
I've looked at my check stubs to check on a check,
I've searched for my tweezers and pulled out a hair,
I've opened a window to let in some air,
I've straightened a picture, I've swatted a fly,
I've shifted the tie clip that clips down my tie,
I've sharpened each pencil till sharp as a dirk . . .
I've run out of reasons for not starting work.[1]

RICHARD ARMOUR

---

[1] Used by permission of the author.

Contents

1

Five Minutes
Is a Long Time

The late Mrs. Eleanor Roosevelt, whose staggering schedule included writing a regular newspaper column, numerous speaking engagements, and participation in both national and international projects, was once asked how she managed to do so much. She simply replied, "I never waste time."[2]

No conscientious pastor wants to waste time. On the contrary, harassed by multitudinous tasks and the frenzied pace of modern churchmanship, he diligently seeks to save time.

Few occupations demand so many hours per week of work as does the ministry. Surveys by *Fortune* magazine and American Management Association show that many top-notch executives work from fifty to sixty hours a week. A poll of clergymen revealed the average minister puts in more than seventy hours every week. Some work eighty hours.

Members of one congregation were asked to indicate on a questionnaire how many hours they felt their pastor should devote per week to each of the following tasks: preparing sermons, personal interviews, administrating the affairs of the church, committee meetings, budget planning and promotion, community activities, youth groups, comforting the bereaved, and advising those contemplating matrimony. Totals on the answers averaged eighty-two hours per week. One member proposed two hundred hours. (A week has only 168 hours!)

---

[2]From "Make Your Minutes Count," a booklet by Dorothy Carnegie used in the Dorothy Carnegie Course for Women.

Feverish activity to assume all obligations with some degree of efficiency has been listed as one cause of ministerial breakdowns. The exhausting marathon of endless, diverse duties, performed against the squeeze of dwindling time, damages like driving a car with the emergency brake on, or frustrates like racing the engine with the car in neutral—plenty of buzzing but no progress. The strain will inevitably show as it did on one nervous executive who, asking his secretary where his pencil was and told it was behind his ear, snapped, "Don't you know I'm a busy man? Which ear?"

Efficiency experts inform us that most people work well below their ability level. Adherence to a simple set of elementary, well-tested, and effective principles will accomplish much more in less time, leaving more hours for reading, planning, and self-development. These suggestions are explained in subsequent chapters.

First of all, we must convince ourselves repeatedly of the value of time. This resolve must become an indelible component of our daily thinking. "Time is valuable. I must not lose it, but use it. I dedicate myself to the task of spending my time as wisely as possible to the glory of God."

Worth of Time

When Benjamin Franklin was working in the back of his store in the room where his newspaper was printed, a customer came in, spent a long time looking at the books, then finally asked the price of one. The clerk quoted the cost as one dollar. The customer, thinking he could reduce the price, insisted on seeing Mr. Franklin, who, though busy as always, thought something urgent merited his attention. Astonished to find a man who thought he would sell the book cheaper than the quoted price, Franklin, to teach the customer a lesson, named the price at one dollar and a quarter. The surprised customer objected, "Why, the clerk said it was just one dollar!"

"True," said Franklin, "and I could have better afforded to take a dollar than to have been taken out of the office."

Thinking Franklin was joking, the customer repeated his inquiry, once more asking the lowest price. This time Franklin said rather severely, "One dollar and fifty cents!"

Openmouthed, the customer exclaimed, "Why, you just offered it to me yourself for one dollar and a quarter."

"Yes," replied Franklin, "and I could better have taken that price then, than a dollar and a half now." The customer left humiliated.

Benjamin Franklin also said, "Dost thou love life? Then do not squander time, for that is the stuff life is made of."

A higher premium is placed on time today than two centuries ago. An eighteenth-century clock in the capitol building in Williamsburg, Virginia, does not possess a minute hand, only the hour hand, like many clocks in that century. People traveling by horseback felt they were on time as long as the lone hand was somewhere near the appointed hour. When railroad service was introduced into rural areas, neighborhood clocks had to have a minute hand added, which had to be kept accurately, for residents discovered that trains ran not only on schedule but left on the minute. Today the term, *7:37 train,* conveys distinct meaning. Maximum deviation from accuracy tolerated in an engineer's watch is thirty seconds in a week.

To do anything worthwhile consumes time. It takes time to get an education. It takes time to learn a trade. It takes time to make a friendship. It takes time for courtship. It takes time to read a book. Too often people want results but do not wish to spend the time to reach their ambition. Said one wife to a mother with her four fine children, "I'd give thirty years of my life to raise four children like yours!" The mother responded, "That's exactly what it cost me!"

Napoleon once told an officer, "Ask me for anything but time. That is the one thing beyond my control." A sign in an office read, "Five minutes is a long time."

The pastor who would save time must have a keen awareness of its value.

Waste of Time

When an officer's revolver accidentally discharged in a police station in Louisiana, the bullet tore into the clock on the wall. The local newscaster facetiously reported that the policeman had murdered time!

When asked what they are doing, many people answer, "Oh, I'm killing time!" What did time ever do to us that we should murder it?

A man who took a plane from the Orient to America wrote,

Lost, Wednesday, February 10th, somewhere over the Pacific Ocean, while flying westward; that does not mean I lost something on that date, but that I lost that date. One moment it was Tuesday, and the next it was suddenly the same hour on Wednesday. We had crossed the international date line. The day was gone for good. True, I have had some twenty-five-hour days and some twenty-seven-hour days to make up for it, but there is something uncanny about losing the day all in one chunk.

Yet some people lose hours every day, and days every month, which cannot be accounted for. How ungrateful for any Christian, redeemed by divine love, to frivolously fritter away his time like a playboy when so much needs to be done for the Lord. The French have a road they call, "The Street of Lost Time."

Time is God-given.—Time should not be wasted because it is God-given. Though others may have more talents, we all have the same amount of time. God gives to all equally. Time cannot be bought, no matter how rich you are. No matter how poor, you won't receive less. The President of our nation, or the board chairman of the largest corporation, has no more time than we. Each of us has sixty minutes to the hour, twenty-four hours to the day, and seven days per week.

Time is fleeting.—Time should not be wasted because it is fleeting. Repeatedly biblical metaphors remind of the brevity of life: grass that withereth, flower that fadeth, tale that is told, shadow that declineth, vapor that banisheth away. Victor

Hugo said, "Short as life is, we make it still shorter by the careless waste of time."

Someone has estimated that in the average life of seventy years, time would be used up as follows:

3 years spent in education	14 years in work
8 years spent in amusements	3 years in reading
6 years at the dinner table	24 years in sleeping
5 years in transportation	3 years in convalescing
4 years in conversation	

The person who attended a ninety-minute religious service each Sunday and who prayed ten minutes each morning would only be giving ten months, not even a full year, out of seventy years. How quickly time slips by!

Time is uncertain.—Time should not be wasted because it is uncertain. Though legitimate to plan for years ahead, goals should be set with the recognition that only if God wills can such projects be possibly executed. We boast not of tomorrow for we know not what a day may bring forth.

> The clock of time is wound but once,
> And no man has the power
> To tell just when the hands will stop,
> At late or early hour.
>
> Now is the only time you own;
> Live, love, toil with a will;
> Place no faith in tomorrow, for
> The clock may then be still.

Time is irrevocable.—Time should not be wasted because it is irrevocable. Mythology represented opportunity as a bald-headed man with a tuft of hair at the front of his head, always moving forward. If a person is to seize opportunity, he must grasp it at the moment it presents itself. Otherwise, it is beyond reach.

In a lost-and-found section of a newspaper appeared this

ad: "Lost, yesterday, somewhere between sunrise and sunset, two golden hours, each set with sixty diamond minutes. No reward, they are gone forever." The dial of time can never be turned back. Once you are in your twenties, you can never be a teen-ager again. Once you hit your fiftieth birthday, you have left your forties forever! Says the hymn writer,

> Time like an ever rolling stream
> Bears all its sons away;
> They fly forgotten as a dream
> Breaks at the ope of day.

America's reduced-hour workweek will prove of no avail if we squander the extra leisure hours. A Chinese gentleman on a tour of an American house listened patiently to explanations of each timesaving gadget. At the end he asked, "And what do you do with all the time you save?"

In reality time cannot be saved. An hour cannot be tucked away for use later. Wise spending, rather than wasting, is the way we save it. Failure to use time in a worthwhile manner will bring regrets like the man who said, "I had a friend I always intended to know better. Yesterday he died."

The late Dr. Henrietta Mears, dynamic Christian education leader, summed it up, "Time cannot be saved; it can only be spent, and if not spent wisely and well, it is wasted."

Wise Use of Time

The scrupulous pastor, realizing that valuable time can be so easily wasted, will resolve to invest it in the wisest employments. The author will never forget a roommate in Bible school. Already a college graduate, Bill was always studying Spanish. Every spare moment he could be seen perusing a Spanish grammar or dictionary. He stayed at school just one year, then headed for Mexico to work with Wycliffe Translators. After two years of labor among a tribespeople, he returned to New Jersey to speak at the Keswick Bible Conference and to be married. His messages at the conference were rich with blessing. Two days before the wedding they found Bill dead. It was revealed that in the two years Bill had been in Mexico he had reduced the dialect of the tribe to writing, had made a dictionary of the dialect, had written a grammar, and then had translated the Gospel of Mark therein—all in two years. Moody Bible Institute later made a movie titled *The Bill Bentley Story*. When Bill stands before his Lord to answer for his use of time, he will stand unashamed. Our aim should be to manage our hours so that we may someday hear the Giver of all time say, "Well done, good and faithful servant."

The saintly Robert Murray McCheyne wrote in his diary, "My heart must break off from all these things. What right have I to steal and abuse my Master's time?"

Charles Cowan, missionary to the Orient, wrote to a friend, "Be spiritually alert. God keep us from duties evaded, capacities wasted, opportunities neglected, the God-given life slipping away from our grasp."

The apostle Paul wrote, "Walk circumspectly . . . redeeming the time, because the days are evil" (Eph. 5:15-16). A few years later the very city where he penned these words was burned. Christians were made scapegoats. Blood ran deep. Not long later Paul died a martyr's death there. No wonder he urged believers of his day to buy up every opportunity to do God's will. Likewise, pastors living in a day of rocket-rattling, international tensions, and gross materialism should seize opportunities to do God's bidding.

R. Kenneth Strachan, director of the Latin America Mission, was visiting the Sunday evening service in a little chapel in Guatemala City. Sitting on the platform waiting to preach, he listened to the reports on the afternoon's activities of visitation and evangelism. A man came to the platform, evidently of Indian background and poor. His face shone as he gripped both sides of the pulpit and began to speak to the congregation. He said that he was celebrating this day. Exactly two years ago the Lord had saved him, completely changing his life and giving him the joy of witnessing for him. "Today," he continued, "I decided to add up all the time of this new life which God has given me to serve him. This is what I found out." Pulling a small piece of paper from his pocket, he started reading the figures.

Two years of knowing and serving the Lord equaled 24 months, 104 weeks, 730 days, or 17,520 hours. The congregation sat up with interest. By the time he got to 1,051,200 minutes and 63,072,000 seconds, rows of Guatemalan faces, many simple Indian believers, were smiling from ear to ear. Faces old and young, with white flashing teeth or toothless gums, were grinning in pure delight. Imagine someone able to add like that! And God so good to give a man all that time.

Dr. Strachan commented, "Somehow I could hear another voice saying, 'Walk in wisdom toward them that are without, redeeming the time' (Col. 4:5)."

Says the poet,

> I have only just a minute,
> Just sixty seconds in it;
> Forced upon me—can't refuse it.
> Didn't seek it, didn't choose it,
> I must suffer if I lose it,
> Give account if I abuse it.
> Just a tiny little minute,
> But eternity is in it.

Someone has said, "Yesterday is a cancelled check. Tomorrow is a promissory note. Today is the only cash you have. Spend it wisely."

2
Put People to Work

"I have never mimeographed a page in my entire ministry," said one pastor. "I do not know how. And I refuse to learn!" He added, "When our church purchased a new duplicating machine a few years back, the salesman offered to teach me how to operate it. Politely, but firmly, I showed him the door."

This pastor's refusal to mimeograph does not stem from any aversion to soiling his hands but from dislike of devoting valuable time to tasks which can be done by members of the church. "When I have been trained to minister the word publicly from pulpit and privately in interview, why should I give precious hours to what many others can so ably and willingly do? I need every minute to study and counsel the souls entrusted to my care."

Dwight L. Moody said, "Put ten men to work rather than do the work of ten men!" Assigning work to ten men multiplies a pastor's time tenfold. One pastor operated on the policy, "I never do anything that someone else can do."

Delegating Work Is a Scriptural Principle

The nonmimeographing pastor was following a biblical principle, even if unwittingly. In the growing early church the Hellenistic element murmured against the Hebrews, claiming their widows were neglected in the daily distribution of alms. The archenemy of the church was taking double aim at the infant fellowship, not only creating dissension, but also turning the apostles from their all-important ministry to lesser tasks. But with divine insight the twelve resisted the temptation, asserting it would be a serious mistake for them to neglect the word of God to wait on tables (Acts 6:2). They solved the problem by having the church elect seven capable, spiritual men to take over the business of alms distribution. Noble and necessary as was table-serving, putting seven other men to work freed the apostles for prayer and the ministry of the word. After the election of these first seven deacons the historian comments, "The word of God increased; and the number of the disciples multiplied in Jerusalem greatly" (v. 7).

Many fine pastors have seen their influence gradually curtailed as their ministries have been sidetracked to table-serving. One influential minister, recognizing that the good is the enemy of the best, took inventory of his activities, then determined to give up membership in most of his clubs—fraternal, civic, and social—which had been subtly eating away dozens of hours monthly. The hours then released for the vital areas of his vocation yielded considerable growth in the church, both numerical and spiritual.

When Jethro visited Moses in the wilderness, he noticed that his son-in-law was wearing himself out by acting as judge for every complaint arising among the people. Perhaps Moses had not delegated authority to anyone because he distrusted the ability of his countrymen so recently removed from serfdom. To save from exhaustion both the time and strength of Moses, Jethro recommended the appointment of subordinate judges who would handle all cases except those too difficult, which would be referred to Moses. So Moses chose capable men to rule over thousands, hundreds, fifties, and tens (Ex. 18:13-27).

When the Lord Jesus fed the five thousand, he worked through his disciples, passing the food to them, who in turn passed it to the thousands. To these same apostles he committed the assignment of dispensing the Bread of life to all nations.

Because he could not shepherd more than one church at a time, Paul arranged for elders to feed and lead the flock in every church. On their first missionary journey Paul and Barnabas had John Mark as their assistant. Mark's performance of minor errands released the apostles for their important evangelism (Acts 13:5). The book of Acts depicts Paul surrounded by a team of younger men whom he was training and sending out to witness in places he could not visit. Luke, Demas, Crescens, Titus, Timothy, Epaphras, Silas, and Tychicus were among the host of helpers whose labors liberated more of Paul's time for his vast preaching and literary endeavors.

When the modern pastor delegates work, he follows in the train of men like Moses, the twelve, Paul, and the Lord Jesus, all of whom saved time by putting others to work.

Decide What Is Major, Delegate What Is Minor

After his heart attack President Eisenhower was forced to curtail his work load drastically. So he decided to schedule fewer appointments and social engagements, and to delegate correspondence and routine matters. Thus he limited himself to paramount issues. Suppose every pastor had to cut his schedule in half. Would he not discover ways of getting others to relieve him of the inconsequential? Asked the secret of his success, one general manager replied, "I worked at essentials, rather than at trivialities."

A physician finally able to relax with a friend late one night confided that seventy-two patients had passed through his office that day. Questioned how he could possibly see so many, he answered, "I didn't see all of them personally. My secretary-nurse handled twenty-four persons—all routine matters like shots or diet data." One third of his work had been delegated.

The top executive in one company had a competent subordinate who screened away everything not properly the chief's business. His detail load was reduced fifty per cent. A questionnaire sent to pastors and church executives indicated that, as in the case of the doctor and the executive mentioned above, one of the best ways to conserve time is to have a good secretary to handle run-of-the-mill details. In most churches the next paid worker added to the staff is a secretary, even though part time. Her very presence in the office to answer the phone, apart from regular secretarial duties, saves the pastor a considerable chunk of time every day by weeding out unimportant calls.

With just so many hours per day the pastor is limited in what he can do. He must select priority projects, then transfer other jobs to responsible helpers. One pastor has never led his Vacation Bible school, instead securing a competent director who took the entire enterprise off his hands. Another preacher has not attended a meeting of the board of trustees for three years. He feels the church has elected competent men who will contact him if pastoral direction is required for any problem. Kenneth Fraser, pastor of a thriving Christian and Missionary Alliance Church in Pittsburgh, says, "I have twenty-two active standing committees. I put lay people to work and delegate responsibilities." When one minister was asked to drive to the next town to secure the license for the church bus, he rightly refused, gently pointing out that this errand fell under the jurisdiction of the bus committee.

Jobs That Can Be Delegated

If a church cannot afford a part-time secretary, the pastor may be surprised at the willingness of capable members to do office tasks. For three years a young stenographer and her girl friend came one night a week to the church office to take the pastor's dictation and file. Much valuable time was saved that minister till the church could swing the services of a paid secretary.

J. Allen Blair, Presbyterian pastor who broadcasts his program, "Glad Tidings," over thirty stations says, "I have sought to find consecrated volunteers to do much of my work. I have a large card file. They have always done my clipping, pasting, mailing, and bookkeeping. People enjoy the work. Why don't we preachers let them do it?"

One minister who broadcasts several times a year has his rough manuscripts typed in finished form by housewives who formerly worked in offices. Another clergyman marks paragraphs he wishes typed, gives the books to volunteer typists who make copies of all marked sections for his files.

Though a few large churches hire research assistants for their pastors, why cannot the pastor of a small church urge his people to be on the lookout for significant articles.

Youth groups and senior citizens provide a wealth of resources. Young auto drivers with new licenses like to run errands, exasperatingly time-consuming for a pastor. Pioneer Girls have helped one pastor on mailings. One Christian Endeavor group takes care of changing the outside bulletin board. Teenagers have assisted with cleaning, house-to-house visitation, and in mowing the church and parsonage lawns.

For five years one eighty-year-old lady prepared the church's weekly mailing which included folding the bulletin, inserting it along with enclosures, plus tying the four hundred envelopes in bundles according to postal regulations. Retired men now find greater utilization in church life. Retired pastors are more frequently called to serve as associate ministers. These tried and proved patriarchs bring a wealth of pastoral experience without any aspiration to usurp the pastor's position. One church employed a retired bank vice-president part time to contact new families in a growing area as well as to call on absentees.

The pastor can save time by having his members visit. The late Leonard T. Lewis, former president of Gordon College, related that when he was pastor of a large church the thousand members were not reaching the community, so he arranged for twenty visitation teams of two each for weekly calling. One team was led by the head of the trustees who apologized that he didn't know how to go about it. Lewis advised, "Just tell them what Christ means to you." First night out the trustee gave a testimony which, though short and faltering, so interested one family that he brought the pastor the following week. As a result the entire family made definite decisions for Christ. Claiming this the most thrilling experience of his life, the trustee continued visitation, thus adding to his pastor's time.

In the realm of mutual help church members can relieve the pastor. Stephen Olford,[1] pastor of New York City's Calvary Baptist Church, points out that members themselves should assume the responsibility for counseling scores of people who then would seldom need to see the minister. He cites Hebrews 10:24-25 as most significantly teaching that it is the duty of the membership to look out for one another, to exhort one another, and to see that one another is regular in church attendance.

No pastor should be saddled with janitorial jobs like arranging chairs or putting out hymnbooks. Nor should he be bothered with minor matters like the frequency of piano tuning, the color of choir robes, nor the type of refreshments at the next social. Nor should he have to count the people present in the Sunday and midweek services. Rather, assigned personnel should report church, Sunday school, youth, and prayer meeting attendances promptly. When a church official passed away suddenly, leaving insufficient time for the congregation to learn the time of the funeral which had been incorrectly stated in the newspaper, the pastor asked one of the church ladies to organize a phone brigade to pass along the pertinent information, which resulted in a large attendance at the service. A lady who has taken a short correspondence course in journalism efficiently handles all news releases for her church.

To save her husband the time of reading lighter periodicals, a pastor's wife can be alert for provocative articles and illustrations, especially if cued in on his advance preaching ideas. Why not let the pastor's wife handle the finances of the home.

---

[1] "What's Happening to Our Pastor?" *Moody Monthly,* January, 1964, p. 20. Used by permission of *Moody Monthly.*

Paying the bills, writing the checks, budgeting the money, and balancing the bank statement all consume precious time. Besides, she may be a better manager. One Christian school president suggested, with tongue in cheek, that wives be given articles which indicate scientifically that they are in better condition to shovel snow than their husbands.

When planning a trip a pastor should have a travel agency arrange his reservations. This saves the time of writing letters, phoning, and sometimes a jaunt to an airport office.

One pastor transfers responsibility to his impersonal wristwatch. Wishing to give undivided concentration to present duty, he owns a watch with an alarm which he sets to sound off just before his next important appointment.

Taking a leaf from the practice of busy doctors, many preachers today suggest that members, unless incapacitated, come to the study to talk over problems, instead of the pastor making house calls. Besides saving the minister's traveling time, this method guarantees privacy for the interview. The pastor should not consume precious moments running to members' homes on the slightest beckon.

Pastoral Sharing of Tasks Is a Divine Plan

One man had a way to handle tramps.[2] When a transient knocked on the door for a meal, the man would point to a pile of wood which he always kept handy, asking him to move it to a new location. When the job was done the tramp would get his meal. Next time another knight of the road showed up the man would have the transient move the pile back to its original spot. In relating this story to a seminary graduate an older pastor said, "Always have a job for your members. When people work in the church, you'll have a successful church!" In general this philosophy is true but with qualification. People should not be put to work for work's sake; they

---

[2]*Handbook of Church Management.* (New York: Prentice-Hall, Inc.) Used by permission.

should be given a job for which they have ability, and which they recognize as a divine challenge.

In his providence the Lord has given gifts to the entire church constituency, not just the pastor. The preacher was never meant to do all the work, for he has neither the time nor the ability. How can the pastor presume to do it all when he is not the recipient of all the gifts. An executive in a philanthropic society commented that he found it difficult to use ministers in his organization because they wanted to do all the work, or dictate how it should be done, rather than lead others in its accomplishment. Instead of the pastor being the big "I," it should be "we." The pastor is not a one-man band. Little men wish to do it all themselves; big men get others to help, giving credit where credit is due. The Head of the church wishes the pastor to share the load with his flock. Ideally, jobs should be spread around for everyone in the membership, not concentrated on a few overworked saints.

Some pastors adopt the "flow" concept of responsibility used by many businesses and some Christian schools. One Christian institution has a presidential board composed of the president and heads of the college, seminary, business, and development offices. Authority flows down through these heads to committees, faculty members, and employees. The prexy deals mainly with his four departmental heads, who in turn deal with those on lower echelons. Likewise, on the return "flow" all matters from subordinate levels are handled by the heads of departments before they reach the president. Most routine matters and minor disagreements never intrude into the president's time. If pastors put this policy into practice, countless time-consuming trivia and petty disputes would never interrupt their schedule.

The Pastor Must Develop Leadership from Among His Members

The four steps in good executive administration are: analyze, organize, deputize, and supervise. Restating these points: survey the problem, design a plan, assign competent helpers, then call to accountability. With reference to the third step, sometimes in business when personnel is needed for a job, an executive will often look for a man with unused ability, perhaps finding someone with not-so-obvious qualifications. Sometimes a task is delegated to a man with a weakness purposely to develop a potential skill. One leader says, "Tell him where to get information, challenge him, but let the worker expend initiative and carry the ball."

In deputizing his helpers the pastor should inspire, motivate, and create enthusiasm. One Sunday school teacher said of his pastor, "He makes you want to do the job." President Eisenhower offered this definition of leadership, "The art of getting somebody to do something you want done because he wants to do it." Wayne Dehoney, Southern Baptist pastor in Jackson, Tennessee, says, "In delegating responsibility, delegate authority too. Don't try to keep your hand on what you delegate to someone else." Supervise, but don't "snooperize."

The process of breaking members into jobs may sometimes involve pain, like teaching your sixteen-year-old son to drive. Training may also demand more work in the beginning, but in the long run greater benefit accrues to both pastor and layman. Harry Hardwick, president of St. Paul Bible College, Minnesota, states that "one of the most challenging areas of pastoral ministry is that of involving other people in the church program. People have more talent than we give them credit for, or opportunity to demonstrate. It does require effort to inspire people."

However, the pastor should not indiscriminately ask anyone for any job. The use of a talent file and Spirit-led consideration are both necessary for proper assignment of tasks. Lloyd Kalland, professor at Gordon Divinity School and for many years its director of practical work, points out a higher attitude to keep in mind in selecting workers.

We certainly ought to solicit help from others, but in keeping with what will best develop their personalities in the Lord. The pastor should so study his people that he will know what might be asked of each. Anything short of this borders on exploitation, revealing that the church is operated as an organization rather than maturing as an organism.

Stewardship includes not only a man's money but the man himself. The pastor contributes to a person's growth when he gives him the right kind of responsibility.

Some work a pastor can never delegate to another. But many assignments can be performed effectively by members of the church whom the Head of the church has called as definitely as the pastor, and equipped for their particular ministry. Every person in the church is the unique bearer of a special commission which can be fulfilled through him, and him alone.

A proper concept of laymen's responsibilities, plus a training program to recruit workers from the membership to assume most of the administrative and promotional work, would free the minister to be preacher, teacher, and shepherd.

For a pastor to stay on top of his work isn't so difficult if he has some helpers to keep the top from getting too high.

3
Plan Ahead

The fence of a famous marksman was covered with a series of rings, in the center of every one of which was a bull's eye. Asked the secret of his skill, he reluctantly admitted that he shot first, then drew the circles later. Sometimes we hit the target without planning, but planning is preferable and time-saving.

Plan Advance Preaching

The preacher who has no advance preaching plan wastes hours every week, scrounging around for a sermon theme or two. How distracting to find Sunday approaching and still wondering whether to preach on the days of creation or the day of doom. Some bewildered preachers actually consume more time selecting a subject than preparing it. But planning pulpit work ahead avoids confusion and eliminates time-wasting.

Is it proper to plan ahead?—Some ministers question the propriety of selecting subjects months in advance. They deem it disrespectful to the Holy Spirit who should lead us from Sunday to Sunday. Objectors quote the words of Jesus, "But beware of men: for they will deliver you up to the councils . . . But when they deliver you up, take no thought how or what ye shall speak: for it shall be given you in that same hour what ye shall speak. For it is not ye that speak, but the Spirit of your Father which speaketh in you" (Matt. 10:17-20). This promise is not for preachers in the pulpit but for Christians under persecution. (Some pastors may think they qualify!) Peter before the Sanhedrin, filled by the Spirit, was told what to say (Acts 4:8 ff. and 5:29 ff.). For those in the pulpit the filling is back a little farther—the mind must be prepared.

If the Spirit can lead the Saturday night before, can he not lead two Saturdays previous, or two hundred Saturdays before? Dr. Douglas B. MacCorkle, president of Philadelphia College of Bible, comments:

Although some preachers believe that the Holy Spirit cannot work except at the last moment, it is certainly intelligent to assume that the Spirit of God has been used to working on a schedule for a very long time. Therefore, the person would do well to find the proper schedule for his year and not fear to revise it as the Spirit teaches him how.

Going through the week wasting time, then casting ourselves on the Spirit at the last moment, may be wicked presumption and an insult to the Spirit.

Advance preparation does not rule out emergencies, special situations, or changes from time to time. The pastor under the direction of the Spirit may be led to break into a planned series at almost any point to preach on some current issue which needs immediate handling, as many ministers did with the Supreme Court ruling banning Bible reading in the school. The preacher is to be master of his program, not its slave!

Advantages of advance planning.—Planning pulpit work months ahead saves time in ways other than reducing hours lost through hunting for a topic or text. It gives direction to the pastor's study, concentrating his reading in a designated area for months before. When the Sunday comes to begin the series, ample time has been expended on research. He can also be on the lookout for illustrations to fit a projected theme. Material will be discovered which otherwise would have slipped by unnoticed, had the pastor's mind not been oriented in a certain direction. Book purchases can be selected more intelligently. Some pastors, intending to speak on a particular book for several months, buy several commentaries on that book. Reading time is better spent through prudent foresight.

Advance sermon development avoids repetition. Dependence on the inspiration of each week results in unregulated discipline that tends to return to pet themes or those on which we feel we possess more knowledge. Repetitious preaching wastes time that could be devoted to new fields.

Some housewives have to go to the store before almost every meal. More efficient housekeepers anticipate their needs for several days, making only one or two shopping trips a week, carefully selecting the best quality at lowest price in minimum of time. Working ahead on pulpit discourses provides better material for sermons with less energy and time. When a preacher has done months of research, his coverage will be much superior and more thorough than had he two or three days to scurry around for spiritual food.

Mrs. Norman Townsend, speaking of her husband's method of planning a year ahead, says,

Only in this way can you be sure you are covering doctrine, stewardship, missions, practical Christian living, plus book studies. The pastor's studying is more effective as he looks ahead. When he finds a clipping on the city of Tyre, he knows he'll be preaching on fulfilled prophecy in August, so files it away. When August comes he has illustrations and ideas all ready. The thinnest kind of preaching is Sunday to Sunday.

Merrill C. Tenney, dean of Wheaton Graduate School, says, "I always try to lay out my teaching and preaching schedule well in advance and to put down notes on the themes which I shall be treating. When the proper time comes for delivery, these notes can be collected, organized, amplified, and are ready for use."

Incidentally, advance pulpit work takes much tedium out of sermon preparation. To have to grind out a production for the swift-approaching Sunday is much more of a chore than working without deadline. Delight rather than drudgery accompanies long-range research. Also if spadework has been well done, pressure is off the immediate Sunday sermon. Rather than start from scratch, the preacher need only pull out his ample material for the coming Sunday and merely arrange in final form.

Helps in advance planning.—Be always planning ahead. Always have one or two series "cooking." One pastor says, "I plan most of my year's subjects while I'm on summer vacation. Practically all my sermons are in series, such as books of the Bible or themes broken down into several topics." Another pastor does his advance planning twice a year: in the summer, and in January. Still another takes a day every four months to plan topics for the next third of a year.

One pastor who does not follow the liturgical year closely keeps folders for special church emphasis, chronologically as follows:

New Year	Independence Day
Passion	Labor Day
Easter	Reformation Sunday
Mother's Day	Thanksgiving
Memorial Day	Universal Bible Sunday
Children's Day	Christmas
Father's Day	

Whenever he comes across material that fits any of these categories, he drops it in the proper file. Though he does not speak on every special day every year, he has built up a backlog of usable, available material, necessitating little or no time for frantic, last-minute research. Usually series are given yearly on the passion of Christ, his resurrection, and his birth.

The preacher who delivers two sermons a Sunday could make one expository, the other topical. By always preaching from a book in the Bible, the preacher would have his advance study cut out for him, as well as always be giving the meat of the Word. If he preached half a chapter a Sunday it would take nearly half a century to go through the Bible.

The major doctrines provide profitable series, one a year, broken down into eight to twelve subdivisions, handled popularly: God, man, Christ, salvation, church, Holy Spirit, angels and demons, eschatology, and the Bible. One minister made the doctrine of man vitally up to date under the theme: "What's the Matter with Man?" From early September to the end of November he covered its various phases under the following titles:

What Is Man?	(Introduction)
Where Did Man Come From?	(Origin and unity of race)
What Was Man Like at the Beginning?	(Image of God in man)
Can We Believe the Story of Adam and Eve Eating the Forbidden Fruit?	(Fall of man)
The Plague of the Human Race	(Sin)
Is Your Upper Story Occupied?	(Constituent elements of man)
Is There Life After Death?	(Immortality of soul)
Will the Dead Rise Again?	(Resurrection of body)
Shall We Believe in Hell?	(Destiny of soul)
What Is Heaven Like?	(Destiny of soul)
God's Most Beautiful Poem	(Summary of man's creation, desecration, and re-creation)

A pastor could read months in advance in the various theological volumes on the proposed doctrine, then break the main points down into popular style with current illustrations.

One pastor reads through the Bible looking for just one subject which has caught his interest. With his notebook open he jots down every reference and comment. Half an hour a day can finish the Bible in four months and dig out one hundred pages of notes. Keeping alert for ancedotes and material on the same theme during the months of advance reading, a minister can come up with a thick file of material which can provide the basis for a series of six to twelve messages. One pastor, practicing this method for years, has given series on the tongue, money, fear, envy, thanksgiving, death, family.

Folders should be kept for individual (as contrasted to series) sermon ideas. As illustrations crop up, or more light shines on the text, these can be filed with other material in the folder. Some sermons grow through the years. Henry Ward Beecher said it took twenty years for one of his sermons to mature. As a gardener keeps a succession of plants growing in various beds, the preacher should cultivate many seed-plots of ideas developing in his file. Time spent on faithful, advance digging among the inexhaustible treasures of the Bible will yield many precious gems of truth.

Plan Advance Church Program

A coffee machine newly installed in an office performed its routine frustratingly. When the coin was inserted, first came out the coffee, then the cream and sugar, finally a paper cup. Many church programs operate in reverse, frequently because they are unplanned.

As the powerful ocean liner *Queen Mary* was furrowing through the Atlantic a passenger asked the captain how long it would take the ship to stop at that speed. "More than a mile before it would halt to a full stop." Then he added, "With a ship like this you have to think a mile ahead." A good executive visualizes things as he would like them to exist five or ten years from now. He plans his work, then works his plan. The builder without a blueprint is wasting time.

Many churches maintain a year's calendar, penciling in special events like evangelistic campaign, missionary conference, Bible conference, Sunday school workers' conference, Sunday school picnic, youth retreat, Daily Vacation Bible school, summer camps, and all men's, ladies', and youth groups. Several churches publish a monthly activity calendar which members can post at home for ready reference.

Business has a pitch for most seasons of the year. In September it's back to school, then Halloween, Thanksgiving, Christmas, and then January sales, Valentine Day, Easter, Mother's Day, Father's Day, graduation, summer sales. Similarly some pastors who do not wish to waste time by hit-and miss programs designate each month, or part thereof, for a specific emphasis. One church stressed the following:

September	Back to Church
October	Sunday School
November	Bible Conference
December	Christmas
January	Music
February	Youth
March	"March to Church in March"
April	Easter and Missions
May	Family (Mother's Day)
June	Family (Father's Day, Children's Day) and Graduation
July and August	Daily Vacation Bible School and Camping

Warning should be given that unless plans are detailed well in advance for each of these emphases, the month will rush upon the pastor to catch him unprepared, nullifying almost completely the value of the program and virtually wasting any time devoted to it. If you have no plan, you are wasting time. If you fail to plan in advance, you are wasting time.

To secure some special, sought-after speakers invitations must be issued over a year in advance. Precious time is frequently squandered by frantic efforts to engage a speaker at a late date.

One pastor and board sit down once a year to fix attendance and financial goals for the coming months, then work to reach these goals. "Our church council," says Robert L. Smith, Southern Baptist pastor of Pine Bluff, Arkansas, "meets for lunch once a quarter to plan the calendar for three months 'tight' and for six months 'loose.' " It is said that H. G. Wells often wrote the final chapter of a novel first to keep the plot from going astray. We fire more accurately when we aim well.

Select the Music in Advance

Another benefit of advance sermon planning accrues to the music department. Given a list of coming topics and texts, the choir director can select appropriate choral numbers and rehearse the choirs for several weeks. One pastor said, "With four choirs and three organists early choice is not only helpful but necessary." Music directors feel that time spent on poorly prepared renditions is virtually wasted.

Planning for Special Speaking Engagements

When a pastor is invited to speak at a service outside the regular church life, such as a summer conference, youth rally, commencement address, Sunday school banquet or workshop, early preparation prevents panicking when other responsibilities crowd in as the scheduled event approaches. One much-in-demand speaker says, "I find that if I immediately determine the Lord's will regarding a message as soon as the letter of invitation is read, or the phone put down, then I both consciously and unconsciously begin development immediately."

Planning for Trips

On the personal side many ministers, scheduled out of town for a convention or speaking date, hurriedly throw together a few things in their suitcase before catching the plane or jumping into the car. To their chagrin they discover on arrival they have left some important item at home, like electric shaver cord or needed pair of shoes. One pastor has compiled a list on an index card of essential articles, from clothing through sermon notes. Kept in his bureau at home, this card is checked off item for item as he quickly but confidently packs. "A stitch in time saves nine."

Plan Delivery of Sermon

A Christian leader asked to speak ten minutes on his particular project went over twenty minutes. He confessed to the pastor later that he had just a general idea of what he would say, and that he had not gone over it before. That same service the pastor then cut his message down from thirty to twenty minutes. He had thoroughly rehearsed it with a watch, so that he not only knew that he had to omit material but which material would best be cut.

To speak a shorter time takes longer preparation. But better preparation not only keeps from pointless digression but saves up to ten minutes per sermon, which for a congregation of two hundred would be two thousand minutes, or a total of over thirty-three hours.

Planning Radio Talks

Invited to broadcast four thirteen-minute radio meditations, a preacher saved time, so he thought, by planning generally in his mind preparatory to transcribing all four at one sitting. However, when he taped the first talk at the recording studio, he discovered to his chagrin that he was just starting his last point when the thirteen-minutes were up. He had to do three more retakes before his talk ended within the time limit. This consumed so much time that he was forced to return at a later date for the other three tapings. Another pastor who transcribed a week later in the same studio for later releases of the same program taped four thirteen-minute messages in the time the first pastor took to do one. By typing his talks and reading them over with a watch in hand, he saved time in the long run.

A well-known office motto reads, "Plan ahead," but the slanting, diminishing, margin-crowding letters at the end of "ahead" indicate that the designer had not planned ahead. Herbert Jauchen, successful businessman and former vice-president of Westmont College, comments, "God would have us organized. If businesses were run like *some* pastors operate their ministry, they would soon fold. All important work must be planned."

The pastor who takes the long view of everything saves time. Someone said, "Planning far ahead helps one get ahead."

4
Make a Schedule

"The best way to save time is the best way to save money—by *budgeting*," points out Dr. Edward Hakes, former seminary president and a professor at Wheaton College. "When you budget time, you discover that you don't have enough time to 'buy' everything (as when you budget money), so you 'buy' with time only those activities worth 'buying.' Without some attempt to budget you waste time and 'buy' activities not worth the expenditure."

The person who says, "I don't have enough time," really shouts, "I am managing my hours poorly!" Given a forty-hour day, we would probably waste more time. The real problem is how to arrange the time we do have.

A Time Budget

Just as we have a financial budget, so should we make up a time budget for tasks of the immediate future. Whereas planning (dealt with in the previous chapter) looks ahead for a considerable period to long-range goals, scheduling (the subject of this chapter) involves handling your work load for an hour, a day, or a week on short-range goals.

Dr. Douglas B. MacCorkle, president of Philadelphia College of Bible, says, "The people who make a schedule and keep revising it, weighing or budgeting every item, are the people who move on that straight line, the shortest distance between two points."

Priority List

A list should be made of all we would like to do in a certain day or week. Henry Ford II gains time by writing down things for as far ahead as a month. Then the list should be revised according to importance, placing priority items at the top, and the not-so-essential at the bottom. Then we should proceed to do those necessary jobs, even if unpleasant. Accomplishment of a task will bring a sense of satisfaction, encouraging us to proceed down the list till the "must" work is done. Then we can tackle the less important.

Someone has said, "We don't *find* time to do what we deem most significant—we *make* it." This is why we say, "If you want a job done, give it to a busy person." A busy person knows how to manage time. When you have a schedule, you don't enter your study desultory or trifling, wondering what to do next. Your work is already laid out for you, waiting for you to dive in.

Dr. William Culbertson, president of Moody Bible Institute, says, "The minister ought to make a list of really important and less important duties. He should get done the former and then face the latter. It seems to me this plan must be a daily one, and it should include devotional and exegetical study high on the list."

Taken for granted is the setting aside of time for prayer. No minister will be genuinely effective apart from time spent in communion with the Lord. Ministers almost universally agree that after prayer, study comes first, demanding the best hours of the day, which for most men is the morning. With mind fresh and heart in tune with God through devotional time the majority of pastors spend two to five hours five mornings a week in meditation and study. Dr. Dick Van Halsema, pastor of Central Avenue Christian Reformed Church in Holland, Michigan, says, "Ideally, I like to keep all forenoons from Monday through Friday for time in the study. The Wednesday morning Bible and Prayer Breakfast for our men begins at

5:45 A.M., and at 6:45 A.M. I can be in my study. This gives me an excellent opportunity to work until noon."

Dr. Hudson T. Armerding, president of Wheaton College, reports that "one very successful minister of my acquaintance is not available each morning from nine to twelve. He uses this interval for his sustained study, and turns out a great deal of work." Dr. R. Paul Caudill, pastor of First Baptist Church, Memphis, Tennessee, goes to his study, which is at home, first thing in the morning. He does not arrive at the church office for appointments till near midday. He tries to safeguard as much as twenty-five hours out of the week for study and sermon preparation. Another clergyman spends three or four mornings a week away from home and office at a place where he can be reached only in emergency and where he does nothing but study, pray, think, and write.

Reader's Digest reports the following story from *Pathfinder*.

The minister who fails to study will soon give himself away: The pastor of a small Detroit church thought some practical joker was joshing him as IOUs began to appear in the offering plate, estimating the value of the sermon. But then one Sunday night the offering contained an envelope with bills equal to the total of the IOUs. After that, the preacher could hardly wait to see how his sermons were valued. Amounts were promised, later paid, varying from five to fifteen dollars. But one Sunday the collection plate carried a note: "UOMe $5.00."

Included in that morning study period is sermon preparation for the immediate Sunday. The specter of two sermons each Lord's Day constantly looms before the average minister. Also time should be devoted to advance sermon preparation, as suggested in the previous chapter. Some preachers take a few minutes each morning to brush up on their Greek by reading a minimum of several verses, then parsing each word and reviewing declensions and verb forms.

A must in any pastor's schedule is reading. The father of the famous Mayo brothers made his sons promise to spend at least one hour a day in medical reading. One of the boys to the end of his life kept a record of the hours and minutes he read. The late Dr. Harold Lundquist, former dean of Moody Bible Institute, used to read one hour daily at suppertime, plus snatches during the day. One Presbyterian minister reads four hours a day, two in the morning and two at evening mealtime. (He was a bachelor!) No minister can afford to fail to read. Reading is a lifeline to a fresh ministry. Someone said, "Readers are leaders."

Afternoons and evenings may be given over to counseling, visitation, interviews, administrative work, meetings, and writing. One pastor says, "I have stated hours and days for interviews in my study rather than have people disrupt a schedule at any time. I also run errands over the noon hour or before dinner, such as grocery buying, haircut, or plane tickets." Another clergyman suggests scheduling interviews with terminal limits, such as from "1:00 to 1:30 P.M." rather than just "1:00 P.M." Though the limit may be exceeded, it gives a strong hint.

Take Inventory of Present Schedule

Timesaving experts recommend that everyone keep a record for one week of what you do during each waking hour. You may be shocked to find several entries like this: "10:00-10:25 A.M.—talked on phone with pastor-pal in next town." "11:00-11:45 A.M—Wife called. Watched baby while she shopped." "2:00-3:15 P.M.—visited a shut-in." "4:00-5:00 P.M.—reading sports magazine, just came in mail." This one-week record will reveal leaks in your schedule. Noting the things that receive more attention than they deserve, you can budget your time to plug such leaks. Phone bills now list length of toll calls. Self-inventory disclosed to a minister that he spent seven hours a week on the phone! Another discovered he was reading too many mysteries. Another determined he had to write shorter letters and make shorter visits. Still another found that he accepted too many chore-boy duties like giving the benediction and invocation at outside organizations, consuming many evenings a month in social wasteland.

Dr. Walter Wilson tells how years ago he took three sheets of letter-size paper, ruled each one for fifteen-minute periods from 6:00 A.M. to 11:00 P.M., then for three days jotted down what he did during each fifteen-minute period. Then he applied three rules to each quarter-hour segment: (1) Did this glorify God? (2) Did this bring a blessing to others? (3) Did this prove profitable to me? Says Dr. Wilson,

I scratched off the time if it did not fit these tests. When I finished, 55 per cent of my time—over half—did not measure up. At the time I was operating a tent factory with two hundred employees, pastoring Central Bible Church with two hundred members, broadcasting daily at 7:00 A.M., and raising a family of eight children. When I saw this record, I completely changed my way of living and found I could do three men's work and not be a bit more tired. This inventory altered the course of my life.

Pythagoras said, "Let not sleep fall upon thy eyes till thou hast thrice reviewed the transactions of the past day. What have I done? What have I left undone?" Ever so often a pastor ought to take account of his schedule. Keeping a record of your time can be as interesting as your bowling or golfing score.

Make Out a Schedule for Every Day

Many live by impulse, doing what they enjoy or feel like doing and postponing the unpleasant or difficult. But this is deadly, for worthwhile accomplishments never come from following likes and avoiding dislikes. An industrialist said, "I can hire men to do most everything but two things—think and do things in the order of their importance." Conscious effort must be made to do things in priority order.

Certain large companies require their young executives to submit by Friday night a plan of activity for the coming week. Every morning a pastor should outline activities for the day. Some ministers keep a file for each day in the week into which they can dip for notations of duties for that day.

Dr. Daniel Fuchs, missionary secretary of the American Board of Missions to the Jews and editor of the *Chosen People,* was given a motto, now sitting on his desk, which reads, "Think! Maybe we can dodge some work." Comments Fuchs,

It is not funny. It is absolutely true. Thinking is the greatest time-saving activity. A few minutes at the start of the day carefully planning my program is the only method I know of getting through the day without becoming irritable and without going through a lot of waste motions. One needs to know what is important, what is trivial, what is convenient, and what is nonsensible. I have also learned that it is best to prayerfully make the important and difficult decisions early in the morning. Since God's compassions fail not and are new every morning, confident trust in our Lord's leading will give the necessary peace that by his grace we are doing the right thing. We will not be spending much time fretfully re-examining our decisions. After all, they are not ours, but his.

Some advocate making the schedule out the night before. Then you'll be already organized for the next day, able to sleep without apprehension over tomorrow. Christian educator Mrs. Norman Townsend says,

I have trouble planning a day in the morning. Things I ought to do don't come to mind. I find the night before I can think of all the things I didn't do, should have done, and want to do. So the last few minutes of the day I make a list of high priority for the next day. I can start right at them in the morning.

One Christian worker has a printed form for each day with three columns of six rectangles each. When a job is to be done he makes a note in a rectangle. After completion he checks off the rectangle. Unfinished items at night are copied over by his secretary on the next day's form.

To select the duties that should come first we need and may have divine help. How significant that following the command to redeem the time comes the verse, "Wherefore be ye not unwise, but understanding what the will of the Lord is" (Eph. 5:17). Direction is available to guide to the important, primary tasks. The next verse gives the source of this guidance, "Be filled with the Spirit" (v. 18). To help us invest our time in the wisest way we have the indwelling Holy Spirit whose enlightenment we should seek.

Relentless Routine

Form habits of doing jobs at a certain time. Thereby you will save minutes you might otherwise waste in deciding what to do next. Also, you'll get started promptly on jobs you dislike. "A job well begun is a job half done." We all have the tendency to put off disagreeable jobs. Putterers are "putter-offers" of something unpleasant. Time is lost because the chore has to be done later anyway.

Doing the same job at the same time makes for smooth functioning and mental rhythm, as illustrated by workers on production lines who go through the same motions. Mrs. Allen MacMullen, daughter of Dr. John R. Rice, relates that in the many years she traveled as pianist for her evangelist father,

he always arrived promptly at his office in the morning, even if he had arrived home just two hours earlier from some campaign after traveling all night. I was always bushed and longed for a half day to sleep late and unpack, but this practice he never broke. Also we had family devotions at the same time every breakfast and no one was excused.

Doing things regularly keeps from time-wasting. One preacher answers his mail every day right after lunch. Another answers his correspondence on Wednesday and Thursday when he has a secretary, though urgent letters are answered at once. Dr. Robert Cook, president of the King's College and former president of the National Association of Evangelicals, gives this advice:

In scheduling activities similar jobs should not only be done routinely but clustered. Don't make a phone call, then write a letter, then study, then another phone call, then another letter. Sort out the different kinds of activity. If you have some telephoning, do several phone calls. If you have some letter writing, do lots of letters. You'll get more done per cubic foot of energy than if you splinter out into everything as it comes. If you turn haphazardly from one thing to another, your mind has to be disengaged, get engaged, disengage, get engaged, and you end up wasting an hour or two saying, "Oh, what do I think about next?"

Set Deadlines

Charles Evans Hughes, who became chief justice of the Supreme Court, allowed himself nineteen minutes for lunch. Waiters in the capital restaurant could set their watches by him. Gladstone lived by a timetable, rarely deviating from it.

Most of us work in low gear, puttering and daydreaming when we imagine we are doing our best. Taking on more work and setting time goals will push us into higher gear. A stiff work schedule brings out one's better side. Extra pressure helps people use time well, and breaks easy-on-self habits. A minister used to drive his daughter to piano lesson early Saturday morning. One day when his wife for some reason took the girl, the preacher noticed that he left for his study ten minutes later than the regular time he left to drive his daughter. The pressure of leaving at a certain minute for the lesson hurried him out earlier.

Many preachers try to have their Sunday sermons ready by Thursday or Friday. Says one, "I make it a rule to be finished by Thursday noon. Then Thursday afternoon and all day Friday I spend in visitation. I make only emergency visits the first of the week." A minister who frequently wrote articles for the religious press always set a deadline for the rough draft, then another date for the final copy.

Pastors should read a minimum of one book per week. To help reach this goal perhaps an aim of fifty pages a day should be set. The pastor who already reads one book a week may wish to fix his sights on two volumes. To do this means rapid reading and good retention. Slow readers can buy books on faster reading.

However, be reasonable, though not too easy on yourself. Schedule just a little more than you have been doing, but not so much that you get discouraged. If you try to dial the phone too quickly the finger slips and time is lost. John Wesley said, "Though I am always in haste, I am never in a hurry, because I never undertake more work than I can go through with calmness of spirit."

What About Interruptions

A minister's time is not his own. Any moment a phone may interrupt with an emergency that will call him away for several minutes to an hour or more from his planned pattern. No minister should be so rigid a perfectionist that he lets himself get upset by unexpected events. Rather he must expect some intrusions which should be regarded, not as annoyances, but simply as God's rearrangement of his schedule.

The renowned Episcopalian rector Dr. Samuel M. Shoemaker, once said, "The ministry is a tension between ordered routine and constant interruption." Commenting that some clergymen are too hard to reach, he pointed out that ministers "must know when to go into low gear and take plenty of time for some one person or family, building something with them that can never come in a ten-minute call."[1]

What about the fellow who has nothing to do and comes to your office to do it? Dr. Robert Cook says,

People used to walk in and say, "Well, I just had two hours to kill here in between trains, so I thought I would come and see you." That used to bother me. Then the Lord convinced me that God sends people your way. So now I say, "The Lord must have brought you here. Let's find out why He sent you. Let's have prayer about it." This does two things. It puts the interview on a different level because God is brought into it. Also, it generally shortens the interview. If a person knows that you are looking for a reason why he's there under God, and if he doesn't have one, he soon leaves for greener pastures. So take interruptions as from the Lord. Then they belong in the schedule.[2]

-----

[1] *The Church Alive* (New York: E. P. Dutton & Co., 1950). pp. 80-81.
[2] "Are You Losing Time?" *Moody Monthly*, January, 1963, p. 32. Reprinted by permission from *Moody Monthly*.

Teach Church to Help Pastor Conserve Time

Publishing to the congregation the job description of each member of the church staff will help members with questions to go to the person charged with the particular area of concern. In addition, the pastor may wish to inform his members of his "study time," "day off," or "time with family." This may be done by announcement in the church paper, gentle hint from the pulpit periodically, sharing the problem with the deacons, or in private conversation.

A good secretary truthfully telling people, "He is in conference" or "tied up just now," will remind folks the pastor's time is at a premium and should not be invaded unless important. Learning the need for making an appointment to see the pastor on less vital matters will point up the value of pastoral hours. However, caution must be used lest the pastor build a wall between him and his flock. Patient forebearance and kindly suggestion may help!

By not lingering in socializing, coffee-drinking visits, the pastor will give a note of businesslike urgency to his vocation. Dr. Lewis E. Rhodes, pastor of Broadway Baptist Church, Knoxville, Tennessee, says, "If a pastor does not fool away his time, most of the people will not ask him to fool."

Learn to Say "No"

A noted concert artist was asked the secret of her success. Her reply was striking, "Planned neglect." She explained that when she first began the study of the violin so many things demanded her attention that after caring for such matters she would then turn to her music. But with the violin getting the tail end of her time, she was getting nowhere fast. So one day she made a decision. She determined to reverse the whole procedure. In her words, "I deliberately planned to neglect everything else until my practice period was completed. That program of planned neglect accounts for my success."

We need to learn how to use the middle two letters of the alphabet: N-O. The pastor should not become the messenger boy of every organization that wants a grace at some dinner or a representative on some committee. Though he must not forget his responsibility to the community, he must evaluate the many demands on his time on the basis of priority. "Don't be a job collector," says California pastor Frank Kennedy. "Remember Paul's pointed advice, 'This one thing I do.' Decide with the help of the Holy Spirit what is to be the main thrust of your ministry, then concentrate on that, and give up time-eating peripheral things." However, the pastor should be willing to accept his responsibility to serve on associational, state, and national boards. If every pastor refused such roles, co-operative denominational efforts would suffer or disappear.

In *How to Live on Twenty-four Hours a Day,* Arnold Bennett says there is no time in the program for spending forty minutes reading the newspaper on the train in the morning. He calls this a waste of precious pearls of time. Something more valuable should be read. Alexander Maclaren advised clergymen to keep newspapers out of the study till after evening dinner. During both the Kefauver hearings and the Army-McCarthy debate a minister said, "It's so interesting. I watch it every day." Only on rare occasions should a minister devote time to radio or TV during the day. Some pastors make it a rule not to watch TV till 10:00 P.M. Stephen Slocum, executive secretary of the American Tract Society, says, "Pruning away unnecessary and unprofitable activities, like cancelling subscriptions to some popular magazines and resigning positions in some organizations, seems advisable action to take once a year, and should be ruthless."

Calls on the phone or in the home should be businesslike. Visits in the home or hospital need not be long. A Christian leader relates how when he had pneumonia two ministers came from a distance to call on him and stayed well over an hour, making him feel worse when they left.

Before calling a meeting ask, "Is it necessary?" Often its purpose can be met by contacting two or three people individually, instead of calling an entire committee with all its time-consuming accompaniments. Don't read every word in the newspaper, nor every sentence in advertising circulars. Give up time-devouring hobbies. Write shorter letters. Some people use small-sized stationery. Mary Margaret McBride is reported to have gone even farther by using postcards for correspondence. Don't be a joiner. Decline invitations. Leave early. Ruskin once asked his friends to consider him dead for a few months because he wanted to work.

A little boy entered the dime store with a half-dollar in his hand. Attracted by the glitter of all the toys, his first reaction was to buy everything within the store and take it home. But his father pointed out the folly as well as the impossibility. Then he helped him select one toy that suited him best. As the pastor faces a multiplicity of tasks which bewilder and surround him, he must, understanding what is the will of God, redeem the time, choose the essential, and say "no" to the less consequential.

5

Be Your Own Efficiency Expert

A coast-to-coast chain of hamburger restaurants conducts a training school where they send young men to study the scientific way to prepare and serve hamburgers. The curriculum includes such courses as *Hamburgerology 202, Don't Spare the Mustard 101A* (alternating with *Catsup 102,* and *Pickles and Onions 302-3*). Laboratory demonstrations supplement regular classroom lectures to teach the art of measuring the specific density of potatoes or squirting the exact amount of mustard or catsup. The restaurant chain finds that this university-style approach contributes much to the success of their hamburgers.

Time and motion experts report that most of us waste up to 50 per cent of our minutes and energy doing things in below-effective ways. Doubtless pastors, by finding more efficient methods, could accomplish two or three times as much without driving themselves to exhaustion.

Layout of Desk and Working Materials

One Christian school field man who visits many pastors remarks, "It takes some pastors several minutes to locate a simple article or piece of information. You should see some desks." One of Norman Townsend's mottoes for timesaving was, "Put it back where it goes. Keep things in their places." Every item requires as much room in one place as another. Put articles in the most convenient spot. Orderly arrangement will save time in both finding and putting away.

A pastor's desk should be functional, even though not as modern as executive desks which hide wastebasket, phone, and trays in the drawers. A desk with one two-drawer file could accommodate all the important current files. In such a drawer one pastor has a file for every day in the week, every month in the year, one for bulletin material, major committees, including deacons and trustees, and financial and attendance reports. Any folder he finds requiring frequent handling can be placed in this two-drawer file.

On the other side of the desk this pastor keeps stationery, a folder on correspondence to answer, copies of letters for which he is waiting reply, immediate and advance sermon preparation files, plus the two or three books he is presently reading. Accessible at his fingertips, without moving from his desk, are most of the material needed for his work. On top of his desk he has a diary, a scratch pad, pen, and a tray for in and out material for his secretary.

Close to his desk is a table holding the telephone, dictating equipment, and typewriter. Also close by are his files. Their proximity saves many unnecessary steps. One pastor had a special desk made with three sides in the form of an unfinished square. The middle side is working area, one side is equipment, and on the other are his books and papers.

In *Eternity* magazine offices in Philadelphia are stand-up desks used by associate editors, and once used by the late Dr. Donald Grey Barnhouse—most convenient for the person whose research demands the scanning of several volumes at once. Oliver Wendell Holmes, Jr., supreme court justice, stood up to work at an old schoolmaster's desk. So have many other men, including William Lever, soap manufacturer.

Books should be shelved by general topic, unless the Dewey Decimal system is followed. One clergyman places all his sets of commentaries together, then volumes on individual Bible books, in order, from Genesis to Revelation. Then he groups all theological sets and doctrinal studies. In the next section he has church history and biography, followed by books on practical theology. Then come philosophy, hymnology, apologetics, cults, and finally all miscellaneous volumes of sermons alphabetically arranged according to author.

By all means the pastor's study should be in the church, not at home. In the parsonage he is liable to domestic distractions like the baby pounding on his study door crying for admittance, or his wife appearing in the doorway with hammer in hand for him to perform some needed carpentry. Also, there is something psychological about leaving the house each morning for work. Because the practice is more businesslike, the pastor will probably leave for work at an early hour like other men. The pastor's family profits from having the study located out of the parsonage, for with greater privacy they can lead a more normal existence.

Simple But Adequate Filing System

Many small businesses fail because of inadequate records. If you don't know who your prospects are, how can you advertise? If you don't know who your debtors are, how can you collect? If you don't know how much capital you have, you can easily overextend your resources into bankruptcy. Accurate records reveal which department yields the biggest profits.

Yet some churches cannot give church and Sunday school attendances for three years ago, or even last year. Nor do they know how missionary giving compares with five years previous. How can such a church discover if it is progressing, or learn its weak points? Or how can it go after new members without some sort of prospect list? How can absentees from the Sunday school be traced if addresses have not been secured? Up-to-date files should be kept on all such records.

Of prime importance to the pastor is material he gathers for sermon preparation. What value will this information have if he cannot readily find it? The fruits of his study should be captured and stored for ready use. A minimum of four types of files is required: (1) organizational, (2) textual, (3) topical, and (4) seasonal.

Folders for every organization and activity in the church should be filed alphabetically. Publicity ideas can be dropped under "advertising." Items for the deacons' board can be filed under "deacons." Reference to this folder readily provides data for the deacons' meeting agenda.

A textual file should include a folder for each chapter in the New Testament and for each chapter, or group of chapters, in the Old Testament. A poem, anecdote, or exegesis that fits a certain chapter can be clipped from a magazine and dropped into the appropriate folder. An article on Rahab and the spies would be placed in Joshua 2, material on Stephen's stoning in Acts 7, an explanation of the gift of "helps" under 1 Corinthians 12.

A topical file would contain folders, alphabetically arranged, on main subjects related to the Christian faith, like *apocrypha, prayer, suffering, witnessing.*

One of the most productive of files is the seasonal, a series of folders chronologically listing the important holidays of the church year, on which in some years the pastor will be preaching. (For list of days see previous chapter.) Faithful filing of all types of material will save hours of time when special-day sermons, topical messages, or expository discourses must be preached.

Find Easier Ways of Doing Things, Avoid Unnecessary Motions

The late Mrs. Eleanor Roosevelt's formula was, "Eliminate unnecessary, slave-of-habit things that fritter away time. Stop doing what you must the difficult way."

Don't accept any task as it is. Analyze its operations. See how others do it. Perhaps you can eliminate one step in the procedure. A pastor discovered that in preparing a sermon he would often copy a quote from a book onto a piece of paper, then later type that quote from the paper onto his final set of sermon notes. Realizing he need not copy the material twice, he henceforth made just a reference to the quote. Then when compiling the final draft he would copy the quote directly from the book.

William Bigger, Christian businessman in New York City, advises pastors to handle mail just once. "Don't pick or choose. Discard envelopes at once." Now and again check incoming mail to have your name removed from lists in which you have no interest.

Dr. J. Oswald Smith, world-renowned missionary statesman, writes one-paragraph letters when possible. Have your secretary sign all letters, except personal or vital correspondence. For special instances where speedy replies are desired, enclose stamped, addressed envelope and underline question(s) you wish answered. Have prefabricated letters for types you write frequently, such as letting guests at church services know you were delighted to have them visit, or following up calls in the home. You can just tell your secretary to send the guest-book letter, or follow-up note.

One church has an interoffice mailbox near the entrance to the Sunday school building. The pastor used to spend several minutes each Sunday hustling around to find officials and committee members to give them notes and letters from his bulging Bible. Now he merely slips them into the prescribed deacons' or trustees' slot. Likewise, committee members can exchange memorandum.

A minister used to file each carbon of his correspondence in a folder bearing the correspondent's name till he discovered that he never corresponded again with more than 70 per cent. Now he just keeps carbon copies of letters to which he wishes reply. These he keeps in a folder marked "Unanswered Correspondence." Once a month he goes through this folder, discarding carbons which have been answered, and noting those yet unanswered. He thus saves both the bother and time of setting up folders for each individual correspondent.

When you make notes, abbreviate or make symbols. A check mark on an article passed to your secretary means you wish it back. A circle means you do not wish it returned. One preacher who keeps a list of all the people he visits also marks the type of visit, *H* standing for hospital, *1* for first-time call, *S* if at study, *D* if merely a door call or short visit, and no symbol if a regular house call.

Dick H. Hall, Baptist pastor in Decatur, Georgia, suggests the following helpful office procedures. "Order office supplies only once each quarter. Designate one person to receive, distribute, and prepare daily mail. Designate one person to receive all incoming calls." Definite assignments and schedule of work make for minimum of overlapping. For example, when the bulletin is edited by a certain day of the week, mimeographed by another, and mailed by a specific deadline, the project works more smoothly. Several pastors suggest the advisability of a business manager or administrator as a time-saver. One minister warns that because individual office procedures vary in changing patterns, an "efficiency expert" in a church office has ruined many a happy staff relationship.

Dr. Lloyd Kalland, Gordon Divinity School professor, who for ten years was book reviewer for *Christian Life* magazine, suggests how to efficiently stay on top of one's reading:

When a book arrives, the table of contents should be thoroughly investigated so that the key chapter or chapters may be found. This in turn will suggest a rapid reading of such chapters which in turn will make for a more rapid reading of the whole book. Also, the author's introduction or preface should never be ignored. Here is where the reader ought to get the pitch of the book.

It isn't necessary to read every chapter in every book. Underlying key words or sentences help retain facts. References to vital information, stories, or statistics can be placed in the files, or checked for secretarial typing and filing.

You may be in a rut! If so, be alert for simple ways to save time and motion, like the housewife who discovered that she could save herself many steps by removing the dirty dishes from the dining room, at the other end of the house from the kitchen, by a movable cart, eliminating trip after trip.

Modern Equipment

TV Guide told of a television star who works in his limousine as he drives to New York City each day from his suburban home. He has a phone and dictating equipment so as not to waste commuting time. The preacher should ask himself, "Am I using the best tools?" He should investigate new methods in office equipment, including dictating machines, intercom devices, and copying machines. One church without a secretary arranged for an answering service for their pastor. Returning from outside duties, he has a record of all who called and why.

Do we use the phone as efficiently as possible. Instead of wandering around some new development looking for an unfamiliar street, why not call the post office for the exact location? If you must make an important visit to someone a mile or more away, why not phone first to make sure the person is home. The time spent on the call would be far less than that wasted in driving the mile or more. If mail is fairly local, answer letters by phone. This saves time and expense, for the cost of a letter dictated to a secretary has been computed as more than a dollar. A pastor who heard that a member had just returned from her mother's funeral two hundred miles away could have called in person to express sympathy but instead phoned his condolences. This saved a four-mile trip to the member who appreciated the call as much as a personal visit. One church visitor who received a long list of all new residents in a growing community found out their phone numbers from Information, called each one, and was able to screen out those of another faith or definitely disinterested, and thus concentrate on the real prospects.

The mimeograph is another machine with timesaving uses. For example, minutes of every committee meeting can be made and mailed to each committee member, thus reminding each of any duty assigned at the meeting. Also, agenda can be mimeographed in advance. Mailed to each member, it will remind him of the meeting and of the topics for discussion.

Dictating equipment is almost indispensable to the modern church, possessing many advantages over shorthand. Dictating equipment frees both pastor and secretary to do their respective jobs at their convenience. In dictating there is no need to slow down or repeat, for it's all there. Changes are easy. The pastor labors under no psychological disadvantage of someone hanging on his every word. No apologies nor embarrassment are necessary. Fixed hours are not required for its use. Ideas need not grow cold because the secretary is not available. Dr. J. Palmer Muntz, for many years director of Winona Lake Bible Conference with its innumerable details connected with the invitation, schedules, arrival, and housing of one hundred preachers during the summer, says, "I did almost all my dictating at night when no stenographer was around. Much time can be saved by using a dictating machine instead of dictating directly to a secretary. It also saves her the time she would spend taking down the dictation in shorthand."

Some pastors take portable dictating equipment in their cars or on planes and trains. Some take their machines on summer vacation and mail discs back to their office. One pastor said that answering mail on vacation by longhand or borrowed typewriter used to consume an afternoon every few days, but use of dictating equipment kept it down to an hour or two a week.

Many preachers dictate their sermons for transcription by their secretary. Some take equipment to libraries which do not permit certain books out and dictate paragraphs into the machine. One minister keeps his machine near his bed so as to capture any thoughts that come in the stillness of the night. During World War II Sir Winston Churchill had four secretaries on hand at all times to take his memos. God's servants should be on their toes for we are engaged in even greater warfare.

Other pieces of office equipment considered essential for saving time by W. Douglas Hudgins, pastor of the First Baptist Church, Jackson, Mississippi, include addressograph, folding machine, electric typewriters, Thermo-Fax copy machine, paper cutter, automatic sealing and stamping meter, tape recorder, adding machine, Kardex files, and for the larger church an electric bookkeeping machine.

Another device, doubtless to find greater usage among the clergy, is two-way communication between car and office. Until recently two-way radio systems used by police and taxis have required expensive equipment and complicated licensing procedures. Now the FCC permits any citizen over eighteen years of age to own and operate his own two-way radio system for business or personal use. Licensing is not difficult nor equipment expensive.

Pastor David B. Kachel of the First Presbyterian Church of Lake Crystal, Minnesota, tells of the last straw that propelled him to secure one of these Citizens' Band Radios:

Having visited a patient, I was leaving a hospital in a town twelve miles from home. At the very time I was going out the front door, another member of our congregation, the victim of a severe heart attack, was coming into the hospital via the ambulance entrance, along with his anxious family. Meanwhile a call had come to my home, seeking my presence at the hospital, but I did not receive the message until I had driven home. I returned to the hospital at once, only to find that the man had died on arrival, and the sorrowing family had started for home, no doubt passing me in the night on the highway.

After a year's use of the two-way radio the pastor reports deep enthusiasm. The set, covering a radius of fifteen miles from his parsonage, has proved beneficial time and time again. Undertakers, doctors, construction companies use them. Why not ministers?

Kill Two Birds with One Stone

The daughter of a clergyman was asked if her father ever preached the same sermon twice. Indulging in a moment's reflection she replied, "Yes, I think he does. But he hollers in different places."

Most preachers give their sermons a second time. Jonathan Edward's famous sermon, *Sinners in the Hands of an Angry God,* was preached to his own congregation without any outward evidence of conviction in June, 1741. A few weeks later, in early July, he preached the same message at Enfield, Connecticut. Attending the area conference of the presbytery, he was called on short notice to preach. Dipping in his barrel, which was the saddlebag, he read this manuscript. The result was a great moving of the Spirit.

The pastor who prepares his sermons well and makes full notes can get double mileage by using them again at other speaking engagements in churches, rallies, or Bible conferences. Invited to give the baccalaureate at some college or seminary, he could prepare the sermon for his own church first. Dr. A. W. Tozer, for many years editor of the *Alliance Witness* and pulpiteer par excellence, was scheduled to give a key message at the Christian and Missionary Alliance Council in 1963. His sudden death just prior to the Council kept him from filling the engagement. However, because his message had been delivered in his own Toronto, Canada, church a week before his passing, the text appeared in the *Witness.*

Throwing away sermon notes after delivery is like throwing investments away. If you have put sweat and study into a message, you should conserve the fruits thereof. Through the years as more ideas for that sermon come to mind, clip them to the notes, so that next time the sermon will be improved.

When assigned a radio talk or a religious article for a newspaper, well-rounded notes of previous messages will provide an excellent base for the talk or article, besides saving hours of research. Who knows but what those sermon notes may be expanded into a book-length manuscript! Not only double distance but triple mileage is possible from some sermon notes well done the first time.

One Christian journalist-pastor often rewrites a story which he has published in one Christian magazine for another periodical, changing the order of the facts and using additional material, getting double duty from his original research job.

When a pastor had three funerals within a week at the Christmas season, he used the same funeral topic for the differing sets of the bereaved with a minor change of emphasis to suit each individual case.

One minister does his devotions in Greek, combining inspiration with review. Another keeps a notebook open during devotions, jotting down ideas that flood his mind. These often later form the foundation for a thought-provoking talk.

Advises one preacher, "I try to run my committee meetings the same night as prayer meeting. Almost every Wednesday after the midweek service some committee meets, whether deacons or missionary or Christian education. This kills two birds with one stone, enabling people to have an extra night at home."

Calling is an area where efficiency planning can accomplish two things at once. Visits should be made to people in the same general area on the same afternoon or evening. Knowing he was to drive his wife on his day off to the city to shop, and knowing he should visit a member in a city hospital, a pastor did both on the same day. Recalling he was to attend a banquet in a nearby town, that he had to transcribe a radio program in a studio in that town, and that he had members in a hospital in the same town, a pastor arranged his schedule so he could visit the hospital, then dash to the recording, then attend the banquet.

Dr. Raymond Buker, professor of missions at Conservative Baptist Theological Seminary in Denver, says, "I have learned to listen to the radio and speeches while I read." Mrs. Ivy Baker Priest, former U.S Treasurer, saves time by using a telephone headset which leaves her hands free for other chores while she talks or waits. Mrs. Eleanor Roosevelt said, "Teach yourself to do two or three things together."

One pastor plays golf on his day off, not only for recreation, but to witness to different men. He claims he gets close to them on the green. Do not businessmen combine business with pleasure by scheduling appointments for luncheon?

A pastor with a heavy visitation schedule drops into some committee and group meetings halfway through, enabling him to make important contacts in the early evening, then enjoy the fellowship later.

By praying through the mailing list the shepherd not only can remember his sheep before the throne of grace, but also have his memory jogged as to the names of absentees or special cases whom he should visit.

Be on the lookout for new and more effective ways to get things done. Be your own efficiency expert!

6
Start Earlier

A cartoon showed a new employee arriving late for work. The hands of the office clock pointed to half-past eight. All other employees were busy at their desks. Evidently his tardiness had become a problem, for his boss was greeting him with this announcement, "Instead of a gold watch in fifty years when you retire, we've decided to give you an alarm clock now!"

A boy said to a man who had missed his train, "It wasn't because you didn't run fast enough. It was because you didn't start soon enough." This is also why some people miss the boat. Promptness in starting work in the morning is a necessary quality in every laborer, even the pastor-employee of the church. Beginning early not only saves time but saves the best time.

Efficiency of the Morning Hours

For most people personal efficiency is at its highest during the early morning hours. Tests on executives using games similar to *Monopoly* showed they made profits early in the day but dissipated them at night. Some organizations forbid policy decisions after 4:00 P.M.

Basal metabolism, that complicated process in which the body burns up oxygen, varies in people, and with it the sense of well-being and mental alertness. Some people rise ready to go full blast immediately, then taper off by evening. President

Eisenhower is cited as an example of this type. Some start slowly to go strong by evening, like President Roosevelt. Some fortunate folks move at full speed every waking hour.

To find your efficiency cycle, it is suggested that you put down the number ten when feeling tops, zero when feeling lowest, giving self an estimated mark for in-between frames of mind. A week or two of record-keeping would show that most of us hit our peak soon after breakfast, decline slowly till late afternoon, then jump forward a trifle after dinner to dwindle down after 10:00 P.M. The average diurnal course of mental capability has been charted as follows:

8:00 a.m.	105%		4:00 p.m.	96%
10:00 a.m.	102%		8:00 p.m.	98%
1:00 p.m.	101%		10:00 p.m.	97%[1]

Our work should be arranged to suit our cycle. For most this would mean tackling the harder jobs, doing the creative tasks, like sermon preparation and decision-making, in the morning. Surgeons perform more operations in the morning for heads are clearer and hands steadier. Magazine and light reading should be delayed till later in the day.

Tests also indicate that at certain seasons the body mechanism operates more efficiently. Spring and fall seem to be top times. Because these seasons fit the church year so well, could not the pastor plan extra work in September to recoup summer-slump laxity, and in March to reconstruct enthusiasm after the winter cold for the passion, Easter, and Pentecost emphases?

Not only do early morning hours permit us our best thinking, but also they may be our only uninterrupted moments. Often these hours provide our only free times for study. Because life conspires against creative contemplation, some executives, instead of locking themselves during regular working

---

[1]Donald A. Laird, *The Technique of Getting Things Done* (New York: McGraw-Hill Book Co., 1947), p. 185.

hours in a secret office with phone disengaged, start before the phones begin to ring. Senator Margaret Chase Smith tries to start each day as early as possible, claiming she can get twice as much done before 9:00 A.M. as after.

Someone said, "There's gold in morning hours. Get up early three mornings and gain one day of time."

The Practice of Many Men in History

Aristotle, philosopher, lecturer, and prolific writer, made a contraption that woke him up at daybreak.

Beethoven arose at daybreak winter and summer to work on musical compositions. Daniel Webster started work at 4:00 A.M. Philosopher Immanuel Kant was at his desk by 5:00 in the morning. The man who succeeded in laying the Atlantic cable wrote down at 6:00 A.M each morning the things he wished to do that day.

Thomas Edison began work by 6:30 A.M., thus completing a couple of hours of labor before most potential inventors had finished breakfast. Isaac Pitman, founder of the shorthand system named after him, developed his method by working before breakfast. Arthur Godfrey believes he saves twenty minutes each day by simply getting up when he wakes up.

Significantly, many Bible characters rose early in the morning, usually to meet God or do his work.

"Abraham gat up early in the morning to the place where he stood before the Lord" (Gen. 19:27).

"Jacob rose up early in the morning, and took the stone that he had put for his pillows, and set it up for a pillar, and poured oil upon the top of it" (Gen. 28:18). There it was he made a vow to God.

"Moses rose up early in the morning, and went up unto mount Sinai" to take the second hewn tables of stone (Ex. 34:4).

Gideon "rose up early on the morrow" to examine the fleece (Judg. 6:38).

Job "rose up early in the morning, and offered burnt offerings" for his children (Job 1:5).

Example of examples, it was said of the Lord Jesus, "In the morning, rising up a great while before day, he went out, and departed into a solitary place, and there prayed" (Mark 1:35).

Many Christian leaders made it a practice to rise early. Martin Luther said, "If I fail to spend two hours in prayer each morning, the devil gets the victory through the day."

John Wesley rose at four o'clock to spend two hours in prayer and meditation each morning. He said, "I have so much to do that I must spend several hours in prayer before I am able to do it."

John Calvin started at 6:00 A.M. Leonardo da Vinci, sculptor, painter, architect, and engineer, climbed the scaffold to start work on *The Last Supper* at dawn.

Timothy Dwight who entered Yale at the age of thirteen, taught there at nineteen, and later became its president for over two decades, used to rise at 4:30 A.M.

Bishop Asbury said, "I propose to rise at four o'clock as often as I can and spend two hours in prayer and meditation."

Department store owner John Wanamaker, who also was superintendent of a large Philadelphia Sunday school as well as postmaster general, was one of the first men to his store in the morning. At the age of seventy he still arrived at 7:00 A.M. to inspect the floor of his stores, either in New York or Philadelphia, confronting sleepy managers with new ideas on their arrival two hours later.

Biographers of Dr. G. Campbell Morgan, prince of expositors during the early part of this century, tell how he toiled incessantly, rising early and retiring late, working all day except for time off for social fellowship among close friends. The crowds that heard his expositions in the pulpit never saw him at 5:00 in the morning with Bible and notebook spread before him.

Perhaps in earlier centuries people retired at night earlier than we do today. When John Wesley was staying at a Methodist institution staffed by three preachers he went to chapel one morning for the 5:00 A.M. service, but none of the ministers showed up. They had been sitting up late the previous night chatting. Wesley ordered a 9:00 P.M. bedtime curfew thereafter for these preachers.

Though the hour of rising and retiring may have been earlier in previous generations, one way to capture more time in our day is to start earlier.

What Should Be Starting Time?

In his book, *The Preacher: His Life and Work,* J. H. Jowett gave this advice,

Enter your study at an appointed hour, and let that hour be as early as the earliest of your business-men goes to his warehouse or his office. I remember in my earlier days how I used to hear the factory operatives passing my house on the way to the mills, where work began at six o'clock. I can recall the sound of their iron-clogs ringing through the street. The sound of the clogs fetched me out of bed and took me to my work. . . . Let the minister . . . be as business-like as the business man. Let him employ system and method, and let him be as scrupulously punctual in his private habits in the service of his Lord, as he would have to be in a government-office in the service of his country.[2]

A survey made among ministers as to suggested starting time for their profession ranged mainly between 7:30 A.M. and 8:30 A.M., with by far the majority suggesting 8:00 A.M. If many high schools start classes by 8:00 A.M., if numerous college courses are offered at 7:50 A.M. or earlier, if many businesses expect employees at 7:30 A.M., a starting hour of 8:00 A.M. or thereabouts is not unrealistic.

Admittedly, some pastors' cycle of efficiency calls for late working and consequently not so early rising. One Christian

---

[2](Garden City: Doubleday, Doran & Co., 1928), pp. 116-17.

leader does his best work from 3:00 in the afternoon till 3:00 in the morning. Another says, "I am a late starter. I don't get to the study before 9:30 A.M. I usually retire at midnight. For me an early start is not the answer, but to work when I feel most creative." One preacher comments, "I find most quiet after 10:00 P.M." But for most ministers more efficiency would result from an early start.

Dr. Merrill G. Tenney, dean of Wheaton Graduate School of Theology, says, "A pastor ought to be in his study for active work between seven and eight in the morning, and should continue at it until twelve noon. Mornings are the best for work." Monroe F. Swilley, Jr., Southern Baptist pastor of Atlanta, Georgia, reaches his desk by 7:15 each morning.

Some preachers study in their office a couple of hours before breakfast, then start office hours at 9:00 A.M.

Dr. Vernon Grounds, president of Denver Conservative Baptist Seminary, by starting his day, as a rule, with a 7:00 A.M. appointment manages to squeeze in from half a dozen to sometimes a dozen counseling sessions every week.

Dr. Paul S. Rees, for twenty years pastor of First Covenant Church, Minneapolis, Minnesota, and now vice-president of World Vision, left for his church study at five o'clock each morning.

Dr. V. R. Edman, chancellor of Wheaton College, says,

I find it imperative to begin the day early in order to accomplish the day's task. Perhaps my wife and I are extremists in that regard. We find it very helpful to arise by four o'clock in the morning, perhaps a little earlier. We have a cup of coffee and a sweet roll or doughnut at that hour, and then take at least an hour and a half for uninterrupted devotional reading of the Scriptures and prayer together. The phone never rings at that time of the morning, and there are no other interruptions. After a bowl of cereal about 6:15 A.M. I am on my way to the office. In addition to the all-school prayer meeting that I lead from 7:00 to 7:30 each school morning I have time to get office work done before the secretaries arrive. Then I can tackle the new day as it develops.

Discipline Needed

Vaudeville performer Harry Lauder used to sing, "Oh, it's nice to get up in the morning. But it's nicer to lie a-bed." A Christian executive who travels much relates, "My work takes me into the homes of numerous pastors. Though many are on the job bright and early, some don't get out of bed much before 8:00 A.M., then loaf around before going to their study at 10:00 or later."

Early rising means disciplining oneself to earlier retirement. You can't consistently have the one without the other. The late TV show or postmidnight social chat may have to be curtailed. Setting one's clothes out the night before will save time in the morning.

Dr. George A. Miles, president of Washington Bible College, suggests the discipline of early rising, at least by 6:00 A.M., to maintain a definite daily schedule of prayer.

In his book, *A Serious Call to a Devout and Holy Life,* the puritan William Law gave this advice:

If you were to rise early every morning, as an instance of self-denial, as a method of renouncing indulgence, as a means of re-deeming your time, and fitting your spirit for prayer, you would find mighty advantages from it. This method, though it seems such a small circumstance of life, would in all probability be a means of great piety. It would keep it constantly in your head, that softness and idleness were to be avoided, that self-denial was a part of Christianity. It would teach you to exercise power over yourself, and make you able by degrees to renounce other pleasures and tempers that war against the soul.[3]

Early rising may require not only an alarm clock but will-power. Pastor Stephen Olford of Calvary Baptist Church, New York, tells of a student at Cambridge who, to get up early each morning, rigged a contraption, so that when the alarm went off a sponge dripped cold water on his face.

---

[3](New York: E. P. Dutton & Co., 1926), p. 169-70.

A young preacher troubled by inability to get out of bed in the morning asked an older parson, "Do you pray about getting up?" "No," came the answer, "I just get up!"

A new Christian asked George Muller, whose faith prayed in millions of dollars to support his orphanage, to pray that he would get out of bed earlier, so he too could pray in the early morning hours. Muller replied, "You get one leg out, and I'll ask the Lord to get the other leg out!"

For thirty-five years Dr. Albert Barnes pastored the influential First Presbyterian Church of Philadelphia. During this time he produced commentaries on every New Testament book, as well as on several from the Old Testament. When he decided to write these books, he wondered how the care of his large parish would permit time for this additional labor. He solved the problem by doing all his writing before breakfast. By rising regularly between four and five o'clock in the morning he spent the hours before breakfast in writing. By nine o'clock he was ready for a full day's work at pastoral duties.

We shorten life by rising late. An old maxim puts it, "The more we sleep, the less we live." If health permits, may not one of the best ways to find time be by appropriating an hour from our sleep? Philip Doddridge calculated that a person by rising two hours earlier in the morning for the space of forty years, supposing he goes to bed at the same hour at night, would add almost ten years of eight-hour working days to his life. What a valuable addition to any man's life!

When Dr. Adam Clarke, author of a well-known set of commentaries on the entire Bible, was a young man, he saw a copy of Erasmus' *Greek New Testament* advertised by a bookseller. Next morning he rose early, went to the book store and purchased the volume. Two hours later another man called to buy the book. "You are too late," said the proprietor. "Too late!" exclaimed the man, "Why, I came as soon as I had eaten my breakfast." The bookseller answered, "Adam Clarke came and bought it before breakfast." His motto was, "Never put off till after breakfast what can be done before."

7
Use Spare Minutes

Called at age twenty-six to the pastorate of a small Baptist church which paid only seventy-five dollars a year salary, William Carey worked during the week as a cobbler to support his wife and two children. Thirsty for learning, he kept beside him as he labored a book for study. In seven years he learned five languages, including Greek and Hebrew. He not only studied textbooks but read every good book he could borrow, among which was a copy of the account of Captain Cook's voyages.

With his mind turned toward the destitute condition of the heathen, he began to crusade for missionary expeditions. Despite firm opposition, including the famous rebuke, "When the Lord gets ready to convert the heathen, he will do it without your help or mine," he persisted till sent out to India at thirty-two years of age.

Before his death he supervised the translations of the Scriptures in forty different languages, spoken then by a third of the globe. Many of the versions he translated himself, retranslating some six and seven times. "He is justly regarded as the father of modern missions."[1]

Referring to Carey's habit of studying while at his cobbler's bench, one historian commented, "If young men and women whose educational advantages have been limited would take

---

[1]Henry C. Vedder, *A Short History of the Baptists* (Philadelphia: American Baptist Publication Society, 1897), pp. 174-79.

but a tithe of the pains to utilize their odd minutes that Carey took, they might do anything they chose."

David Livingstone, likewise, used odd moments to study. His hours in the factory were long, from six in the morning till eight at night. From the factory he rushed to night school where he studied from eight to ten. Then he did homework till midnight or later. He also took a Latin book with him to the cotton mill. In this way he read through classical authors like Virgil and Horace.

Successful executives are "minute-minders." Productive people use those waste minutes that invariably crop up in even the busiest schedules. This explains why busy people, given additional jobs, get them done. They know how to milk every minute out of the day. In addition, proper use of idle moments reveals a positive outlook on life. Those who keep turning over critical thoughts and rehashing lost battles make for unhealthy attitudes, but the person who converts spare minutes into constructive thinking will be a happier individual.

Secular World

The best seller, *Cheaper by the Dozen,* relates the story of the late Frank Gilbreth, engineer and pioneer in the science of motion study. He and his wife used timesaving methods in family life as well as in business operation. They raised their twelve children on the principle that time is a great gift to be used productively, not frittered away. Even when brushing their teeth in the morning they learned languages from large lettered cards placed in the bathroom by their father.

Strauss wrote one of his famous waltzes on the back of a menu while waiting for his meal in a Vienna restaurant. Harriet Beecher Stowe grasped a pencil between her teeth while kneading bread dough, so that during in-between moments she could write snatches of *Uncle Tom's Cabin.* One popular song was composed while the writer was caught in a traffic jam.

Businessmen often sign letters while talking on the phone.

While waiting to see the manager of a company, a salesman asked the secretary at the outside desk if he could use the phone. He made several business calls, some to competitors of the firm whose reception room and phone he was borrowing.

The *Reader's Digest* told of a woman's success school which requires its students to keep track of time spent riding buses, standing in supermarket lines, sitting under driers, waiting for food to cook, or sitting early in PTA meetings or concerts. Then the students discover how reading, learning a foreign language, sewing, deep-breathing exercises, and planning menus can all be blended into the "frozen minutes" of each day.

Mrs. Eleanor Roosevelt wrote many of her newspaper columns in the spare minutes that intervened between conferences, interviews, and appointments. She also kept stationery with her at all times to write letters while traveling.

Dressing

George Muller used to pray while he shaved each morning. Should not the Christian, commanded to "pray without ceasing," capture some odd moments for communion with God?

Generally considered the founder of the card system of Bible-verse memorization, the late Dr. Oscar Lowry, evangelist, teacher at Moody Bible Institute, and author of *Scripture Memorizing for Successful Soul-Winning,* tells how he came to use this method.

When I entered school to take a course of training for Christian service, I found myself in possession of a lazy mind. I had been following a trade for a few years and my mind had not been subject to discipline along this line. As a makeshift, I filled the fly leaves of my Bible with such references as I would need for personal work, and when dealing with an individual I would turn to this list to find what passage to use to meet the particular needs in each case. I determined to overcome this poor, lame way of doing personal work and to overcome the inertia of my own mind.

Rising early the morning after making the resolution to memorize Scripture, I chose for my first reference a rather difficult passage of two verses. It was no easy task to get these verses fixed correctly in mind. But I was determined to win the victory, so wrestled with the passage until completely mastered. The second morning, while dressing, I memorized an additional passage and thoroughly reviewed the one learned the previous day. The third morning I memorized still another, carefully reviewing the other two. I kept adding a new passage or two each morning, and each day meticulously reviewing all memorized before.

When I had memorized seventy-five passages, I began to review some of them weekly instead of daily. Later I looked over verses only once a month, then every three months, then half a year, then annually. If I failed to repeat a verse correctly I put it back into the daily review.

By this time I was using cards, writing the full verse on one side and the reference on the other. One advantage of cards is that they can be kept on the desk, workbench, dresser, automobile, and thus reviewed anywhere.[2]

Before too many years had passed, Dr. Lowry could quote from memory more than 20,000 of the Bible's 31,175 verses. He once said, "If a person would spend ten minutes each morning in Bible memorizing, in a year he would have devoted six days of ten hours each."

Lunch

Few executives enjoy the luxury of a casual lunch in some fine restaurant unless they intend to talk business, have a board session, committee meeting, keep an appointment, sell, promote, or consult. Some businessmen find it timesaving to eat in the office, avoiding an extra half-hour delay in crowded restaurants.

In his autobiography Benjamin Franklin gives an account of an arrangement he made with his brother, to whom he was apprenticed, that the might gain more time for reading and study.

I . . . proposed to my brother, that if he would give me, weekly,

---

[2](Chicago: Moody Press, 1932) pp. 40-46. Used by permission of Moody Press, Moody Bible Institute, Chicago, Illinois.

half the money he paid for my board, I would board myself. He instantly agreed to it, and I presently found that I could save half what he paid me. This was an additional fund for buying books. But I had another advantage in it. My brother and the rest going from the printing-house to their meals, I remained there alone, and, despatching, presently my light repast, which often was no more than a bisket or a slice of bread, a handful of raisins or a tart from the pastry-cook's, and a glass of water, had the rest of the time until their return for study, in which I made the greater progress, from that greater clearness of head and quicker apprehension which usually attend temperance in eating and drinking.[3]

The faculty of one divinity school eat quick lunches in the office of one of the professors, chatting relaxingly about theological problems and academic matters. Many Christian organizations sponsor luncheon meetings or serve dessert to help visitation teams and Sunday school workers get to their tasks more quickly. One pastor, whose wife and school-going children eat early lunch, reads *Newsweek* at his midday meal, usually taking four or five noons to go through it.

Waiting for Supper or Appointments

One minister listens to taped Bible passages for reflection while waiting for the dinner call. A pastor known for his prodigious correspondence says,

People often wonder how I can keep in touch with so many by a mere postal card. This I do waiting for the dinner bell to ring. This usually involves five or six letters besides. Another secret is to write two or three cards while your wife is finishing dressing to go out to some church event. It is amazing how much can be accomplished in this way.

Robert L. Smith, Southern Baptist pastor in Pine Bluff, Arkansas, sends approximately one hundred birthday cards a month. He signs these personally, while talking on the phone.

---

[3]*The Autobiography and Other Writings of Benjamin Franklin,* (New York: Dodd, Mead & Co., 1963), p. 23.

A clergyman who has several committee meetings to attend each month makes it a point to join the meeting when his presence is more vitally required later on. He works in his study to the last minute, assigning someone from the meeting to alert him when needed. He also joins the many church social functions half-way through or in their final minutes, thus conserving the valuable, earlier evening hours.

Always Have a Book with You

Daylight Saving Time is an effort to save an hour of daylight for outdoor activity. Moment-saving time can capture several minutes a day for profitable reading. With a crying need for more time to read, pastors can add to their regular, scheduled period for reading by snatching odd moments here and there. Diligence in this practice will double the number of books read. One pastor manages two a week, or one hundred a year. The public press recently reported that a chemist has to read two hundred thousand pages a year just to keep abreast in his field.

By taking advantage of spare minutes, one clergyman managed to plow through Latourette's massive seven volumes of church history, while keeping up on other books as well. Seizing enough time to read fifteen pages a day, five days a week, he completed a volume every six weeks, and the entire set in less than a year. An extra ten minutes a day of reading would total sixty hours in a year, enough to read the Bible through or most of Shakespeare's plays.

Raymond McAfee, for many years associated with the late Dr. A. W. Tozier, well-known Christian and Missionary Alliance pastor, author, and editor, reminisces:

During his early Christian years he read widely in everything. . . . He often likened himself to a hungry bee gathering nectar from any flower. He was never without a book, and in later years that was usually a devotional classic or a hymnal—or a ten-cent-store spiral notebook in which he jotted ideas of his own for books or articles or editorials. During the years I knew him, he never owned a car, so on many occasions I drove him to appointments or to a restaurant for a meal. We would no sooner be in the car than he would be reading to me—Watts, Wesley, Eckhart, Fénelon, Faber, Guyon, Burns, Shakespeare, Keats, Byron, Wordsworth, Milton, Emerson, to name a few authors. He would read a few lines, put the book on his lap and comment for a while.[4]

One pastor reads snatches of books in the following situations: in the dentist's waiting room, before his children's recitals or school programs, in bed, in his car waiting for funeral processions or wedding rehearsals to begin, seated in the ladies' shoe department while his wife shops, standing in line at the bank, waiting for the car to be fixed, between meetings at conventions, on the subway, sunbathing on the beach on his day off, and in the barber shop. A missionary said, "I made it a habit to read as I walked the jungle paths of Burma." Pastor Clarence Hayden of Peekskill, New York, once forgetting a book he had been reading in the barber shop was questioned by the barber about the book, which led to a discussion that brought about the barber's acceptance of Christ.

Dr. Dick Van Halsema says,

I find by using a local library I can discipline myself into keeping abreast of books outside the theological field. For example, I get two books from the library and try to scan or read them before they are due. When I return them on the due date, I take home another pair of books. This reading must be done in spare moments.

Socrates said, "Employ your time in improving yourself by other men's writings; so you shall come easily by what others have labored hard for." Reading is one of the minister's lifelines. He should always have books handy for odd moments.

Traveling

John Wesley, who used to read in the saddle, urged young

---

[4]From *The Alliance Witness*, New York, N. Y.

circuit-rider preachers to do the same. Bishop Francis Asbury read one hundred pages of good literature daily. His saddlebags were packed with books. While riding he taught himself Latin, Greek, and Hebrew. Wesley even wrote in the saddle.

Though easier to read in the saddle than in the driver's seat of today's high horsepowered auto, many ministers redeem time when driving. One city pastor clips verses to the dashboard of the car to memorize when stopped for red lights or traffic jams. One Christian businessman has a dictaphone in his car to dictate correspondence. One wife says, "My minister-husband has limited time to read all the religious literature that comes to us, so whenever we are in the car together, I generally take along some magazines and read to him various articles of interest."

A missionary executive says, "Rather than listen to all the junk on the radio, I get the news and then pray around the world for the many missionaries in our society, especially for their recent requests." Many ministers on long trips take books to read at brief stops or coffee breaks. Dr. G. Douglas Young, director of American Institute of Holy Land Studies in Jerusalem and Hebrew scholar, carries with him on his extensive travels little cards containing Hebrew vocabulary and idioms which he faithfully reviews.

Other clergymen find driving one of the best times for just plain thinking. Says one, "While driving, some of my best ideas, including sermon themes, come to me." Some think through a problem. On a long, lonely overnight drive one pastor's creative meditation helped give his Sunday school a victory in a national contest. A Bible college president keeps a pad of paper on the seat because his mind works better in motion, walking or riding. Flowing thoughts jotted down can be organized and analyzed later. Testifies one Christian college professor, "Using traveling time to penetrate problems makes driving or public transportation an experience of value instead of frustration."

Perhaps we need some of the enterprise of the young lady on the subway who awkwardly removed the kerchief from her hair as she hung to a strap. When a passenger offered her his seat she declined, pointing to the fan spinning over her head, "I'm drying my hair."

Abraham Lincoln reportedly wrote the Gettysburg address on the back of an envelope while gazing out the window of a railroad coach—not day-dreaming, but meditating creatively. One peripatetic preacher says, "I work every moment on a plane, reading, writing notes." Dr. Merrill C. Tenney says, "I do a great deal of book reviewing while traveling." The late Dr. Donald Grey Barnhouse, pastor of Tenth Presbyterian Church in Philadelphia, could frequently be seen in a crowd of people at New York City's Pennsylvania Railroad Station, waiting for the door to the track to open, avidly reading a book, or bending over his portable typewriter as he wrote an editorial for *Eternity* magazine. He used his portable typewriter regularly in waiting rooms, on trains and planes.

Before Church Services

Dr. Richard S. Beal, over forty years pastor of the First Baptist Church, Tucson, Arizona, enthusiastically comments that "saving time has been a hobby of mine all through a half-century of my ministry." Among the many devices he uses for utilizing precious moments is personal work prior to services. He says,

Much personal contact is done prior to Sunday school. Mrs. Beal and I have made it a habit of getting to Sunday school at 9:00 A.M., and thus able to meet the incoming pupils and often deal with them. Then we work among the congregation for fifteen minutes before the morning and evening services and are able to deal with numbers of people. Often we retain folk following a service too.

Relaxation

Even during times of relaxation many ministers get things done that do not demand highest mental concentration. Watching TV, some do hobbies of stamps or coins, light reading, conditioning exercises, and write letters.

One Christian magazine editor, who led a busy life, used to proofread between plays and periods at football games. One pastor, who takes in two or three big-league baseball games a year, always brings a book to peruse before the game and between innings.

Pastors' winter retreats and summer conferences provide a relaxed atmosphere where pastors not only unwind but learn in short-term courses in Bible, journalism, Sunday school, youth methods, and music.

For thirteen summers a noted Baptist seminary professor turned from theology to enjoyable reading of the major poets. But he never lost sight of his calling. At the end of that period, Dr. Augustus Hopkins Strong gave to the world the fruit of his vacation meditation, a volume titled *The Great Poets and Their Theology*.

D. L. Moody used to read the Bible through intensively every summer. He said, "I get tired toward the end of July, and I go away to the mountains. I take the Bible with me." He commented that reading it through made it a new book, rich and varied, with new truths flashing from hundreds of unexpected and undiscovered points. He referred to that summer reading as "tuning the instruments."

A large percentage of clergymen use part of their summer vacation to plan the coming year's pulpit ministry and church program. This sound practice saves time, puts some of the holiday period to excellent use, and gives direction to the ministry of the coming months. Leisure time need not be idle time.

Enforced Delays

During his imprisonment John Bunyan wrote nine books, including *Pilgrim's Progress*.

A listener was much impressed by an address given by the

late Dr. Robert Speer in Baltimore in 1941 on the theme of Paul's use of the titles of Christ. He was more surprised by his extemporaneous delivery from the Greek New Testament. But what amazed the listener most was the story behind the sermon. Over forty years earlier Dr. Speer, in his work among students, was traveling by train through the Allegheny Mountains when a severe blizzard covered the tracks and stalled the train. The passengers took refuge in a nearby village until the tracks were opened twenty-four hours later. While most of the people killed the weary hours with complaint, card games, or fitful sleep, Speer seized the opportunity to do something he had long wished. He put most of those twenty-four hours into an intensive study, in Greek, of Paul's use of the titles of Christ found in his epistles. This study laid the basis for wider study on the subject and his memorable sermon.[5]

When the architect of a European cathedral came to insert the stained-glass windows he found himself one window short. Frantically he wondered what could be done. An apprentice in the manufactory where the windows were made solved the problem. Collecting the fragments of the glass cast aside when the windows were made, sorting and studying them, he finally produced a window that harmonized with the others. Some thought it the most beautiful of all. Likewise, some men make their finest attainments from bits of time that have been broken from the edges of a busy ministry.

A bank motto gave this advice, "Take care of the pennies, and the dollars will take care of themselves." Pastors could well adapt it to read, "Take care of the minutes, and the days will take care of themselves."

---

[5]W. Reginald Wheeler, *A Man Sent from God* (Westwood, N. J.: Fleming H. Revell, 1956), p. 167.

8
Take Time Off

Dr. Paul E. Adolph,[1] medical examiner for several missionary societies and former medical instructor at Moody Bible Institute, tells of a minister who came to his office in nervous exhaustion, boasting that he had taken no vacation for ten years.

He labored under the conviction that his work was of such importance that he could take no time off. But he had come to the place where he could neither relax nor sleep. Though modern treatment was prescribed, it took him almost a year (equivalent of a month's vacation for ten years) before he could actively participate in his work again.

Because a person engages in the Lord's work doesn't grant immunity from the laws of health. Every minister should plan periods of relaxation.

Age of Speed, Frustration, and Breakdown

Someone commented, "What America needs is fewer seventy-mile-an-hour roadsters and more rocking chairs." A lady told a stewardess to ask the pilot to please not fly faster than sound because "I want to talk." A husband rebuked his tardy wife, "If you hadn't been so slow we would have caught that train!"

---

[1]*Health Shall Spring Forth* (Chicago: Moody Press, 1956), pp. 95-96. Used by permission of Moody Press, Moody Bible Institute, Chicago, Illinois.

She retorted, "If you hadn't hurried me so, we wouldn't have had to wait so long for the next one!"

Someone said, "Not only do we live at a fast rate but we even die suddenly." Our speedy generation has been described by this anonymous doggerel:

> There was a young lady named White,
> Whose speed was faster than light;
> She left home one day in a relative way
> And came back the preceding night.

This frenetic pace has permeated Christian work. One theological professor said, "The communion of saints has become the commotion of saints, and St. Peter has given way to St. Vitus." Meetings are multiplied ad infinitum. When someone remarked to a minister sentimentally that there would be no partings in heaven, he quickly replied that he hoped there would be no meetings.

An anonymous piece asked, "What Does A Pastor Do?" Then came the answer.

The pastor teaches, though he must solicit his own classes. He heals, though without pills or knife. He is sometimes a lawyer, often a social worker, something of an editor, a bit of philosopher and entertainer, a salesman, a decorative piece for public functions, and he is supposed to be a scholar. He visits the sick, marries people, buries the dead, labors to console those who sorrow, and to admonish those who sin, and tries to stay sweet when chided for not doing his duty. He plans programs, appoints committees when he can get them; spends considerable time in keeping people out of each other's hair; between times he prepares a sermon and preaches it on Sunday to those who don't happen to have any other engagement. Then on Monday he smiles when some jovial chap roars, "What a job—one day a week!"

According to a psychiatrist who treats missionaries and ministers, number one health problem among Christians is depression. Describing his experiences in treating students in a Bible school, the doctor said that in many cases cause of depression was traceable to lack of adequate sleep, nourishing food, or protection from bad weather. They felt something was wrong with their spiritual lives, when in reality they were violating God's natural health laws.

Too frequently we feel we must be on the go every moment. One minister, noted for his close calculations, operated a small farm. One day he observed a worker sitting idly by his plow while the horses took a much-needed rest. The clergyman's sense of economy was shocked for he was paying the young man seventy-five cents an hour. So he said, "Wouldn't it be a good idea for you to have a pair of shears and be trimming these bushes while the horses rest?" "That it would," replied the young fellow agreeably. "And might I suggest, your reverence, that you take a peck of potatoes into the pulpit and peel them during the anthem!"

There are times when we must take time off. All advice in previous chapters about hard work, advance planning, scheduling of duties, maximum efficiency, early starting, and judicious use of spare minutes, must be balanced against the need for periodic, complete relaxation, adequate exercise, and sufficient sleep.

Periodic Rests

Muscles keep healthy through periods of contraction followed by periods of relaxation. This cycle helps maintain the health of the human body. The bow kept under constant tension soon loses its resilience. The person, even a servant of God, who never lets up in his work develops overfatigue which so easily produces disease symptoms.

Some ministers who never take a vacation point out that Satan never rests. Since when do we make Satan our example? Rather we should look to Jesus Christ who one day said to his busy disciples, "Come ye yourselves apart into a desert place, and rest a while: for there were many coming and going,

and they had no leisure so much as to eat" (Mark 6:31). Someone commented on this command, "It's either come apart and
rest awhile, or rest awhile or you'll come apart."

Some could have objected to Jesus' order to holiday by
pointing out that people were fainting like sheep without a
shepherd, that wolflike scribes and Pharisees were devouring
the flock, that so much healing and teaching needed to be done.
If someone had asked, "Does Jesus take his followers on a
vacation, holiday, or excursion?" Spurgeon would have answered,

Rest time is not waste time. It is economy to gather fresh
strength. Look at the mower in the summer's day, with so much to
cut down ere the sun sets. He pauses in his labour—is he a sluggard?
He looks for his stone, and begins to draw it up and down his
scythe, with rink-a-tink, rink-a-tink. Is that idle music—is he wasting precious moments? How much he might have mowed while
he has been ringing out those notes on his scythe! But he is sharpen-
ing his tool, and he will do far more when once again he gives his
strength to those long sweeps before him. Even thus a little pause
prepares the mind for greater service in the good cause.

Spurgeon also pointed out,

Fishermen must mend their nets, and we must every now and then
repair our mental waste and set our machinery in order for future
service. To tug the oar from day to day, like a galley slave who
knows no holidays, suits not mortal men. Millstreams go on and
on for ever, but we must have our pauses and our intervals. Who
can help being out of breath when the race is continued without
intermission? Even beasts of burden must be turned out to grass
occasionally; the very sea pauses at ebb and flood; earth keeps the
sabbath of the wintry months; and man, even when exalted to be
God's ambassador, must rest or faint; must trim his lamp or let it
burn low; must recruit his vigor or grow prematurely old.

Spurgeon added,

It is wisdom to take occasional furlough. In the long run, we shall
do more by sometimes doing less. On, on, on, forever, without rec-

reation, may suit spirits emancipated from this "heavy clay," but while we are in this tabernacle, we must every now and then cry halt, and serve the Lord by holy inaction and consecrated leisure Let no tender conscience doubt the lawfulness of going out of harness for a while, but learn from the experience of others the necessity and duty of taking timely rest.[2]

One preacher thought he was redeeming the time when every Sunday afternoon he worked feverishly on his evening service and church matters till twenty minutes before evening service, then dashed two blocks to the parsonage for a quick bite, then rushed back to enter the pulpit just a minute before starting time. Becoming nervous and dizzy, he decided to quit his afternoon labors an hour earlier. Relaxing in an easy chair, plus a slow, modest bit of nourishment, made him a much more effective preacher on Sunday evenings.

Rest Each Day

Did it ever occur to you that the recurrence of mealtime three times daily might be nature's way of giving a break from your work? Anything beyond light reading or pleasant committee meetings at mealtime encourages nervous indigestion.

Many health experts suggest a short break, two to three minutes every hour, such as a short walk down the hall to another office, or stretching. Coffee breaks have their wisdom, if not overdone.

Lying down for a few minutes after lunch gives recuperative refreshment. One preacher has rested after the noon meal for over twenty-five years. Reclining on a couch fully clothed, he has conditioned himself to go right to sleep and to awake automatically in ten or fifteen minutes, reinvigorated as if he had slept for hours. In the earlier years the development of this discipline required an alarm clock in a pail to rouse him from sound sleep. He lists one disadvantage. If he is at some

---

[2] C. H. Spurgeon, *Lectures to My Students* (London: Marshall Bros., 1906), II, 174-75.

meeting or event which precludes a quick postlunch nap, he suffers from sleepiness for a short while.

One minister, who stopped work at 10:00 P.M. but found it difficult to get to sleep, overcame his insomnia by relaxing for an hour with light reading or sports or mysteries on TV, followed by the news and weather. Daily routine should include sufficient hours for sleep to perform its healing work.

A quiet devotional time, not only in the morning but at noon and evening, or oftener, may soothe a tense, troubled soul.

> We mutter and sputter,
> We fume and we spurt;
> We mumble and grumble,
> Our feelings get hurt;
> We can't understand things,
> Our vision grows dim,
> When all that we need is
> A moment with Him.

A painting in the Louvre shows a plowman kneeling in the sod. Behind the praying workman is an angel at the plow. Our plowing never suffers from time spent with him.

The perennial problem with clergymen is how to find time for their families. Partial answer would be to devote a period after the evening meal to the children, which would also furnish welcome diversion before resuming the responsibilities of the evening.

Relax One Day a Week

Every preacher should loaf one day a week. Most rest Monday after the hectic duties of the previous day. Some store up energy for Sunday by taking off Saturday, which also enables them to spend time with the children who are out of school. Others take a half-Saturday and a half-Monday. The busier a pastor is the more imperative this weekly change becomes. Though Christians observe the first day of the week in honor of the resurrection, and not the seventh day as kept in the Old Testament period, many Bible scholars believe that the principle of one-day-in-seven for rest and reverence is eternal and God-given.

The Israelites who failed to rest from agricultural tasks as commanded by the Lord thought they were saving time by using it to store up more grain for their barns. After several centuries of sabbath-violating they suffered seventy years of captivity in Babylon when they couldn't work their land. God is not mocked. Because the sabbath has been abrogated, ministers cannot work seven days a week with exemption from penalty. Unless they relax a day per seven overwork will catch up with them. The minister too needs the calmness of a day off. An explorer who tried a forced march through the jungle with a bunch of savages found that, though incredible speed was registered for two days, on the third morning the natives wouldn't budge, sitting and looking very solemn. The chief explained, "They are waiting for their souls to catch up with their bodies." Busy ministerial life needs a day a week for ragged spirits to recuperate.

Said Spurgeon,

A day's breathing of fresh air upon the hills, or a few hours' ramble in the beechwoods' umbrageous calm, would sweep the cobwebs out of the brain of scores of our toiling ministers who are now but half alive. A mouthful of sea air, or a stiff walk in the wind's face, would not give grace to the soul, but it would yield oxygen to the body which is next best.[3]

This one day a week may involve some hobby. One wife says, "My husband is a devout advocate of proper use of leisure time. He is an ardent artist. He loves God's hills, streams, and woods. To escape the hectic activity of ministerial life he finds peace of mind and soul through paint brushes." Perhaps a pastor, though working his hobby mostly one day a week,

---

[3]*Op. cit.,* p. 172.

could snatch a few minutes in its enjoyment each day, but he must be careful not to overdo it. One missionary on furlough said, "Our pastor has a workshop in his basement. He is very handy. Recently he made a grandfather clock and a trailer. But I'm afraid he is spending too much time down there, several hours each night. We didn't take in any new members this year." What should be a relaxing pastime should not mushroom into an excessive pass-time.

The pastor may wish to indulge in mild physical activity on his day off, like golf, swimming, or calisthenics. One seminary president, feeling sluggish some years back, began to exercise at the YMCA once or twice each week, plus walking for a half-hour each evening during the supper hour. Immediately he felt better and worked with more alertness.

One evangelist bought a small ranch and horse, explaining, "Riding is very pleasant recreation for me for I grew up in a saddle in Texas. I suspect that as hard as I work I may live longer, as well as happier, because of the exercise and relaxation."

One compensation of the ministry is the freedom to alternate activities. After a morning of concentrated study and early afternoon in administrative problems, a pastor can change pace by leaving his study to go out on visitation. One New York City Christian worker tries to find some good reason to walk several blocks at noon each day. Some pastors deliberately walk up hospital stairs instead of using the elevator and park their cars at the other end of the parking lot to provide mild exertion. However, the minister should not overdo his relaxation period, like one who was seen two hours every summer morning on the local tennis courts.

Vacations

Some pastors try to take off an extra day or two every few months. Doctors tell us that to get full value out of time off we need a minimum of two days, for it takes the first day to unwind. Pastors rarely get two days in a row, so they should arrange for periodic breaks. A doctor told a nervous pastor, "Arrange to get away to a convention every now and then." A minister who hadn't bothered to attend annual national conventions or semiannual state meetings found his dizziness and high blood pressure appreciably lessened by attendance at these functions. In fact, some ministers do not take their full month vacation at once in the summer, but divide it into three parts, two weeks in the summer, then one in the fall, and one in the winter or spring.

A lawyer who later became a supreme court justice was a tireless worker. Taking a few days off before an important trial, he was chided by a colleague for loafing at a crucial time. Replied the lawyer, "I need the rest. I find that I can do a year's work in eleven months, but I can't do it in twelve."

Missionaries worn out by deputation meetings and last-minute details usually revel in the leisurely boat trip over calm ocean and under peaceful sky. After Paul's first missionary journey through Asia Minor where he had been harassed and stoned, he returned to Antioch by boat, instead of tedious overland trek. The sea voyage doubtless refreshed him. Picture the little vessel, slowly sailing. See on deck a man bruised and weakened physically. But the quiet restfulness of the trip recuperates his strength.

When Leonardo da Vinci was doing his famous painting, *The Last Supper,* observers were critical of the long periods he would just sit in the cloister and meditate. When they remonstrated about his failure to be about his work, he replied, "When I pause the longest, I make the most telling strokes."

Pauses from intensive periods of hard work will refresh, cultivate radiance, help us laugh at self, free us from oversensitivity, fill us with gratitude, renew us for our daily work, and enable us to make our most telling strokes.

9
Do It Now

Napoleon supposedly had a system for answering letters. He let all his incoming mail pile up for thirty days. At the end of that period most of it had answered itself, or did not need a reply.

A modern counterpart, a clergyman, said, "I never read my mail. If it is important they will write again." However, most pastors consider it a moral obligation to read and answer mail in reasonable time.

How easy to put things off. Though it takes no longer to do something the very first day, preachers, no different from average people, find some reason to delay. They resemble the sailor who argued himself into postponing leaving harbor,

> There are, unless my memory fail,
> Five causes why we should not sail:
> The fog is thick, the wind is high;
> It rains; or may do, by and by;
> Or any other reason why.[1]

Benjamin Franklin had this motto, "Have you anything to do tomorrow? Do it today!" He shocked his folks one day when, after helping salt down the family supply of meat for months ahead, he remarked, "You could save yourself a lot

---

[1]Frederick C. Gill, *In the Steps of John Wesley* (New York: Abingdon Press, 1963), p. 205.

of work later if you would just say one blessing over the entire lot now, instead of at each meal."

Though sacrilegious in that particular context, the suggestion "do it now" can be a potent time-saver in a minister's life.

Tackle Your Work Vigorously

Delays make the job seem bigger than it really is. Thinking about it steals time you could be using to get the job done. A seminary president said, "The work I put off one day usually gets detoured several days." Pushing jobs aside for another day piles up several little tasks which together slow you down and frustrate.

Don't be a deadline worker! Some people note the farthest possible deadline, then wait till the fatal hour approaches before feverishly pitching in. What a miserable way to live—always under pressure and worriment.

How much better to start in ample time. Stay on top of your work. Finish your sermons by Thursday or Friday. Have that article written for the newspaper several days in advance. Life will become more relaxed.

So start your assignment with vim. Don't stare at it, nor mope over it, nor ponder it. Just begin! The minute one man hears a prayer request or makes a promise to pray for something specific he does it immediately, right then and there bowing his head. Dr. Donald McKaig, vice-president of Nyack Missionary College, who for many years carried the triple occupation of professor at Nyack, pastor of a thriving church, and writer of a weekly Sunday school lesson, gives this advice, "For years I made it a practice to do things I had to do as quickly as possible. I started this in college. I did most of my studying before the last minute. If you have something to do, do it. Don't postpone it."

To overcome the habit of putting things off, four suggestions are given. The first step is to decide to break the habit today. Second, discover some things can be put off—the secondary and less important. Third, list the duties that take top priority.

Fourth, tackle with vitality the first item on the list, then on down the jobs one by one. Dr. Harold Lindsell, associate editor of *Christianity Today* and former vice-president of Fuller Theological Seminary, operates on the thesis that "one can never get up enough steam for all the jobs that need doing. So I remember that all I need to do is tackle one item at a time. And how quickly all of them are finished!"

Decide Trifles Quickly

A pastor had room for one more announcement on his coming Sunday bulletin. All important notices were in. How would he fill up the remaining space: mentioning a special speaker six weeks away, attendances at last Sunday's services, or a reminder to people to read the Bible every day? The pastor dillydallied ten minutes before making up his mind. The inconsequence of the decision did not merit that time.

A businessman had these letters in a large frame, "PITTOT."[2] They meant, "Procrastination is the thief of time." Indecision over trivia is a waste of time and brain. Quick decisions are more likely to be right as well as save time.

> Procrastination, thief of time,
> Monster in my breast;
> You would steal God's gift sublime;
> Rob me of Heaven's best.
>
> W. D. JONAS[3]

Answering Mail

Strange as it may seem, some pastors let letters go unanswered for weeks. How much easier and in the long run timesaving to reply the same day or within a few days at the most. Dr. Paul S. James who supervises the expansion of Southern Baptist work in the New York metropolitan area says, "My present program is helped greatly by answering

---

[2]Laird, *op. cit.,* p. 158.
[3]Used by permission of the author.

mail soon after receiving it." Some pastors who receive only one letter a day requiring attention may wish to wait a few days till they can answer several at once. Some reply on two days a week, perhaps when a secretary is available. The value of dictating equipment shows itself at this point, for a pastor can answer mail immediately. Even though not transcribed for a day or two, the mail is finished as far as he is concerned, except for signing.

One Christian editor makes it a rule to dictate an answer to every letter as he reads it. Those requiring more information are placed in a special folder for immediate attention and answered later that day. One Christian businessman advised,

Don't be a paper shuffler. Don't hold on to letters and reports. Do something with them. If not needed, toss out. If a reply is expected, answer. Note if more information is required for later answering. But don't simply lay a paper aside to come back to it later to mull all over again. Handling is time-consuming.

One minister makes it a point to fill in every recommendation form the minute he opens it, such as reference for a member's employment or college enrolment. If a superintendent hands him 30 Sunday school promotion certificates or 150 VBS attendance diplomas, he plows into the monotonous task within minutes, perhaps combining signing with phone calls.

Reading and Filing

When a sentence or a paragraph in a book catches your attention as worthy of capturing, mark it immediately for reference for your files, or for copying by your secretary. If you fail to mark it, you may spend precious minutes thumbing through the pages trying to relocate, or racking your brain to recall which book. One pastor has his secretary type all marked sections in duplicate, then files in two separate places, perhaps one under the text it illuminates, and the other under the most appropriate topic.

Some pastors keep every copy of every magazine to which

they subscribe. This practice devours precious space with material most of which is never used. One minister used to save his periodicals till summer, then read them to clip thought-provoking articles and illustrations. But after a few summers of carting a boxful of magazines, laborious reading which consumed much of his vacation time, plus hours necessary on his return to file the clippings, he decided to read all magazines within a day or so of arrival, file clippings immediately, then toss out the magazines. Many pastors thus dispose of magazines quickly.

Time used to clip and file is well invested. The long view saves time. Perhaps at the moment a precious minute or two is spent, but months later when an apt illustration is needed for the Sunday sermon, the preacher will not have to waste time hunting. "He who hesitates is lost." So is the illustration. Again, the decision where to file a striking story or poem should be made quickly. Should the anecdote fit a verse in a book currently the basis of an expository series, the item should be dropped in that chapter file.

Promptness

Punctuality has been defined as the art of wasting only your own time. Meetings should be started on time. When a singer arrived late for rehearsal, the director exclaimed, "Madam, you are late. You have taken from these ladies and gentlemen that which Almighty God won't restore to them—their time!"

Have a terminal point for ending a meeting as well as starting. Ministerial luncheons which drag on two hours or more could learn from the Lions or Rotary Club which concentrate lunch, business, and address into an hour and fifteen minutes or less.

One advertising executive limits all conferences to an hour, actually setting an alarm to ring. He explains that matters that demand more than an hour for discussion and decision are too big for group deliberation and need individual solution.

For visitors who tend to overstay try these suggestions. At the outset announce the appointment time as 3:00 to 3:30 P.M. As the deadline approaches, set another date. Or, find another person to handle the visitor. Or, slowly rise and gently say, "Does that answer all your questions?" Or, "It has been nice seeing you," or frankly, "I have another appointment in a few minutes." Dr. K. Owen White, former pastor in Houston, Texas, and former president of the Southern Baptist Convention, advises, "Get people to come to the point in personal conferences and close with prayer when you feel the time has come to conclude."

On-time-manship, advertised by a major airline as one of its selling points, is a quality that will save minutes, eventually hours, and perhaps even days.

Jot It Down—Carry a Notebook

Victor Hugo kept a little pad beside him day and night. Heinz of soup fame jotted down the famous slogan "57 varieties" in his pocket notebook while riding a New York City elevated train. Called one of the most time-conscious persons in the world, Henry Kaiser alotted himself five hours for sleep each night, which he called his "idea period," and always had a pad and pencil next to his bed.

The multitudinous details required in pastoral life demand ready recourse to a notebook. As church dismisses, the minister may be told of someone's illness, asked to secure a special tract, given an address change, or invited to talk over a spiritual matter. Unless a genius, he dare not trust his memory. If he makes no notation, he runs the risk of missing some vital duty. "Weakest ink is stronger than mightiest mind."

Flashes of inspiration often cross the preacher's mind. If he fails to jot down his thought, he may forfeit it forever. Dr. Merrill C. Tenney suggests

carrying a pad of paper in one's pocket on which to write down the fleeting ideas that otherwise might be lost. Ideas do not occur at stated intervals, nor in regular periods assigned to them. They usually come when we are thinking of something else. It is a good thing to put down one's notions as they occur, then assess them later. I have found this a helpful procedure. Transferring the thoughts to cards 4" x 6", I now have a fair library of such cards. Often they give me exactly what I want when I want it, because ten years ago I thought of something that is now relevant.

Now Is the Time

How easy to think that some day we will use our time to better advantage. The seminary student says that after ordination he will find time to do his prime duty. He discovers that in the ministry he is constantly beset by the temptation to let peripheral matters crowd out his primary obligations. He will find alibis. "I need a better place to work." "People bother me and keep me from getting things done." "I'm doing too much already." "I'm too busy to read." "My next pastorate will be different." Managing time and going on a diet have one thing in common—talking about it gets you nowhere. Don't wait till you have more time for you have now all the time available at this point. You must start now doing what should be done, and keep on. The truth is that we do with our time pretty much as we want to.

John Wesley for 53 years after his heartwarming Aldersgate conversion went anywhere and everywhere across England preaching the gospel. He was master of six languages and thoroughly versed in theology, history, and literature. Physically he was unimpressive, standing five feet four inches tall, weighing less than 130 pounds. But with seemingly boundless energy he preached 40,000 sermons, traveled 250,000 miles, mostly on horseback, wrote 440 books and pamphlets. His audiences sometimes numbered 20,000 which he held spellbound without public address system. When he died at the age of 87, who would not agree that Wesley had used his time to the glory of God?

Psychologists tell us we can do much more than we realize. Thus we should ever be evaluating and reevaluating. Where should my time go? Am I doing what God called me to do? What should be eliminated? What should get higher priority? Alexander Maclaren, often called "monarch of the pulpit," spent the first twelve years of his ministry in obscurity in a little English town, then went to Manchester where he reigned as master pulpiteer for forty-five years. Maclaren often spoke of the twelve inconspicuous years as valuable preparation for what later became his important period. "The trouble with you young men," he said to a group of seminary students, "is that on graduation you get pitch-forked into a prominent position, and you cannot resist the temptation to attend this tea-meeting, serve on that committee, when you ought to remain in your study and do there the work that is of first importance in serving your day and generation according to the will of God."[4]

A Daily Miracle

Like Israel's manna in the wilderness, the supply of time is a daily miracle. Every morning God fills your purse with twenty-four hours of raw gold for your own spending as you wish. Time is among the most priceless of possessions. Another beauty about time is that you can't waste it in advance. The next hour, week, month, year, are waiting ready for you unspoiled.

The average minister puts in long hours fully aware that "no one ever became the man of the hour by watching the clock!" Fascinated by his job, he enjoys what he is doing, unwilling to trade the privilege of his high calling for any other position in the world. He realizes he is God's servant to be used where God has placed him, a man of destiny come to the kingdom for such a time as this. To execute his ministry he wants to use the minutes, days, weeks, months, and years at his disposal to the glory of God.

---

[4]John Pitts, "Alexander Maclaren: Monarch of the Pulpit," *Christianity Today,* June 5, 1964, p. 7.

Redeem the time! O man of God,
Like polished arrows fly thy days;
Soon will thy pilgrim path be trod,
And then thou wilt stand, for blame or praise,
Before the Throne of Majesty Sublime.
Therefore, O man of God, redeem the time!

Redeem the time! Yea, buy it up
As merchant seeking precious gems;
Each moment is a golden cup,
Thy days are costly diadems.
Though early pleasures lure with merry chime,
Sell not, nor spend, but still redeem the time!

Redeem the time! With lavish hand
Then may'st thou purchase lasting wealth;
As in the hourglass falls the sand,
Thy soul will grow in spritely health.
If thou would'st know, in heaven's fairer clime,
A blest eternity, redeem the time.[5]

J. C. MACAULAY

When managing editor of *Vision* magazine, Larry Ward wrote of his mother's last letter to him. Just back from her funeral at Christmas time, 1957, he leafed through a stack of mail. In the midst of sympathy cards and thoughtful notes from friends, he found a card that was different. It was a birthday card from his mother, containing the last words she had written her son just before her sudden stroke. Eagerly he scanned the personal note she had penned on the back. Commenting on the busyness of the Christmas season, she ended, " I must make the time count this week."

Says Ward,

I carry those words on that little card with me everywhere I go. And over and over again I thank God for one priceless gift He gives us, a gift which comes to us from a royal source each day of our lives, bright and sparkling, absolutely untouched, unspoiled.

---

[5]Used by permission of the author.

What is this gift? The priceless gift of time. Each day we receive a fresh, new supply—24 hours, 1,440 minutes, 86,400 seconds. Twenty-four hours we have never lived before—twenty-four hours we shall never live again.

What a wonderful way for a pastor to face each new day, week, or month—"I must make the time count for the Lord."